More Educators' Praise for
Mindful Teaching and Teaching Mindfulness

"Many teachers often sense there is a mysterious element to their teaching, something that impacted their effectiveness even more than the material they were offering. This book reveals that element, and offers many specific ways to cultivate, harness, and incorporate it. **A must-read for those interested in the potential of education.**"—Soren Gordhamer, author of *Wisdom 2.0*

"This book offers concrete strategies for being less stressed and more emotionally balanced, and present in the classroom. Practicing these techniques will improve any teacher's ability to deal with the myriad of situations that challenge teachers every day. It is **a gift to the education profession and to teachers, learners, schools, and our communities.**"—Suzanne Vitullo, ESL teacher

"A rich resource for teachers, school counselors, and faculty involved in preparing the next generation of educators. **I can't wait to share this book with my colleagues and students.**" —Susan Theberge, Ed.D., professor of education at Keene State College

"**A must-read for all educators.**"—Dr. Thomas Farrell, former school superintendent, Kennebunk, Maine

(over)

"Offers hands-on tools, exercises, and insights tempered by the voice of experience that help to build relationships with students and engage them in learning, and that **will renew teachers' own energy, passion, and commitment.**" —Eugene C. Roehlkepartain, vice president of the Search Institute

"The lessons this book has to offer are simple and easy to relate to yet **important enough to affect the way you choose to live your life.**"—Kristina Weller, elementary school teacher

Mindful Teaching and Teaching Mindfulness

Mindful Teaching and Teaching Mindfulness

A Guide for Anyone Who Teaches Anything

Deborah Schoeberlein
with **Suki Sheth, Ph.D.**
Foreword by **Stephen Viola, Ph.D.**

Wisdom Publications • Boston

Wisdom Publications
199 Elm Street
Somerville MA 02144 USA
www.wisdompubs.org

Library of Congress Cataloging-in-Publication Data
Schoeberlein, Deborah R.
 Mindful teaching & teaching mindfulness : a guide for anyone who teaches
anything / Deborah Schoeberlein, with Suki Sheth ; foreword by Stephen Viola.
    p. cm.
 Includes bibliographical references and index.
 ISBN 0-86171-567-5 (pbk. : alk. paper)
 1. Reflective teaching. I. Sheth, Suki. II. Title. III. Title: Mindful teaching
and teaching mindfulness.
 LB1025.3.S385 2009
 371.102—dc22
                                          2009027151

13 12 11 10 09
5 4 3 2 1

Cover design by Phil Pascuzzo. Interior design by TLLC. Set in Caslon
11.5/15.5.

Wisdom Publications' books are printed on acid-free paper and meet the guide-
lines for permanence and durability of the Production Guidelines for Book
Longevity of the Council on Library Resources.
Printed in the United States of America.

♻ This book was produced with environmental mindfulness. We have elected
to print this title on 30% PCW recycled paper. As a result, we have saved
the following resources: 24 trees, 8 million BTUs of energy, 2,311 lbs. of green-
house gases, 11,132 gallons of water, and 676 lbs. of solid waste. For more information, please visit our website, www.wisdompubs.org. This paper is also FSC
certified. For more information, please visit www.fscus.org.

We hope this book serves teachers and students, in school and beyond school, and all those whose lives they touch.

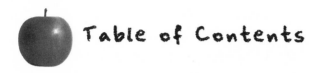

Table of Contents

Foreword by Stephen Viola   xi

Preface   xiii

CHAPTER 1: TEACH AS YOU LEARN   1

    Take 5: Mindful Breathing (for Teachers)   14

CHAPTER 2: MINDFULNESS IN THE MORNING   17

    Noticing Thoughts (for Teachers)   27

    Noticing Feelings (for Teachers)   28

CHAPTER 3: ON TO SCHOOL   35

    Take 1: Mindful Breathing (for Students)   45

CHAPTER 4: HOW YOU SEE IT   53

    Mindful Seeing (for Students)   64

CHAPTER 5: KINDNESS AND CONNECTIONS   71

    Kindness Reflections (for Teachers)   81

    Kindness Reflections for Loved Ones (for Teachers)   82

CHAPTER 6: BEADS ON A STRING   89

    Drawing the Mind (for Students)   93

Mindful Eating (for Students)   97
Noticing Thoughts (for Students)   106
Noticing Gaps (for Students)   107

CHAPTER 7: BODY AWARENESS   111
    Walking with Awareness (for Students)   117
    Mindful Walking (for Students)   120
    Mindful Walking—Attending to the Body
    (for Students)   121
    Mindful Walking—Developing Awareness
    with Distraction (for Students)   122

CHAPTER 8: MINDFUL WORDS   131
    Mindful Journaling with Take 1 (for Students)   134
    Journals and Mindful Seeing (for Students)   136
    Kindness Reflections (for Students)   141
    Mindful Speech (for Students)   147

CHAPTER 9: FULL CIRCLE   157
    Analytical Meditation on Satisfaction (for Teachers)   164
    Short Reflection on the Day (for Teachers)   169

Appendix 1: Summary Encapsulation   177
Appendix 2: Formal Instructions
    and References to Informal Activities   179
Index   197
About the Authors   203

Foreword

MINDFULNESS AND EDUCATION are beautifully interwoven. Mindfulness is about being present with and to your inner experience as well as your outer environment, including other people. When teachers are fully present, they teach better. When students are fully present, the quality of their learning is better. It's a "win-win" equation that can transform teaching, learning, and the educational landscape.

Mindfulness helps teachers in multiple ways by supporting emotion management, reducing stress, and focusing the mind. These skills are essential for career success and satisfaction. With nearly 40% of teachers leaving the profession after five years, we know that the familiar approaches aren't adequate when things get tough in the classroom.

Focused awareness, as cultivated through mindfulness, also helps students by improving attention, promoting academic achievement, reducing problem behaviors and increasing enthusiasm for learning. But the greater educational potential of mindfulness goes beyond raising test scores. Mindfulness has much to offer as educators address other intractable problems of education through facilitating the flexible transfer of skills and knowledge to new contexts, developing deep understanding of student motivation and engagement, strengthening critical and creative thinking, and fostering more self-directed learners.

Tapping into the potential of mindfulness begins when teachers and students learn to pay attention to the *experience of paying attention*. Since teaching stems from personal experience and understanding, educators' familiarity with mindfulness must precede implementation of student-centered methodologies.

The point is that we have to go first—and this book, written by a longtime educator who "gets it," shows how.

Stephen Viola, Ph.D.
Director, Transition to Teaching Program
University of Missouri–St. Louis

Preface

Some people need to know their goal or they can't search at all. For others, though, the quest itself is enough.

Gerald Morris, *The Quest of the Fair Unknown*

NEARLY TWENTY YEARS AGO, I taught a class on HIV prevention as a visiting specialist at an urban middle school in the Northeast. The students were street-smart seventh graders who clearly questioned whether they had anything more to learn about sexual decision-making and disease prevention. While their health teacher stood nervously at the back of the room, the students sized me up.

One girl noticed my maternity clothes and saw an opportunity to test me. She raised her hand and asked, "Well, so, it looks like you're gonna have a baby...and, um, that probably means you had sex and didn't use protection...right?"

It was a teachable moment the likes of which I'd never imagined. There was enormous opportunity there—and also the potential for the entire class to derail. My face burning, I took a deep breath and paused, collecting my thoughts, centering myself while the students' buzz of "I can't believe she said that!" and "Ooh! What's the teacher going to do now?" quieted.

"Yes," I said, "that's how it usually happens when you plan to have a child." Everyone laughed. Then, once the tension diffused, I drew their attention to the link between staying healthy as a teen and having options as an adult. We discussed responsibility for our own health and well-being, as well as that of others. Real-life relevance, in the form of my seven-months-pregnant figure, was right there in front of them. They got the point.

I got the point too—though, of course, it was different from theirs. I had dabbled with meditation, and that experience had unconsciously primed me to notice what was happening—inside me and among the students—as soon as the girl asked her question. I experienced myself standing in front of that class with all eyes on my belly. *(This feels really intense.)* I felt the impact of thirty students' perceptions and unspoken questions about a typically taboo topic. *(There's a lot of energy in the room right now.)* I noticed that I had the ideal opportunity to teach with my words, my physical presence, and my emotional response. *(Take a breath, focus.)*

In the moments before I spoke, as I breathed and waited for quiet, I noticed the quality of my inner thoughts (scattered), feelings (uncomfortable), and physical sensations (flushed) as well as the students' reactions (amusement combined with an increased willingness to take both the class, and me, seriously) and behavior (direct gazes, along with some laughter and squirming).

I noticed all these things without becoming wrapped up in any of them. I felt multiple emotions, but focusing on my breath helped me witness them without reacting unconstructively. I knew that responding to the girl's question in a calm, gentle, and kind manner would convey a powerful message about protecting health, making responsible choices, and caring for others.

By switching my attention to my breathing and opening my awareness to what was happening, I could better manage my own emotions, reactions, and pedagogical response. Doing so positioned me to meet my students' needs and capitalize on this intense—and very teachable—moment. I didn't need to manage their *behavior*, because they shifted their attention and adjusted their own actions in response to my example.

The discussion that followed was transformative for everyone. There were clear boundaries—I was the teacher and they were the students—but we were also "in sync." We were all there, *really there.* They understood the relevance of classroom learning in real life, as expressed by my belly. I understood that teaching modeled *being in the moment* and could infuse the classroom with openness, presence, and caring. And I came to see that students learn as much if not more from *what* we *do* as teachers and how we *are*, than from what we *say*.

That was my first direct experience of mindful teaching in the classroom.

A second illuminating moment came in a sex education class with high school students whose behavior had already put them "at risk" for a range of undesirable health outcomes. These sexually active students had already "been there, done that" and were skeptical of my assertion that, except for cases of abuse or assault, everyone has some degree of control and choice about sex. They'd comment dismissively, "That's not true—sometimes it just happens."

Everyone knew that the "it" was sex, and the "happens" referred to the absence of an active choice. They weren't talking about abuse or assault; rather they viewed having sex as an acceptable default option associated with certain conditions and situations, like being drunk or high. Sex-by-default was also a frequent outcome of "leading someone on" or having the feeling that "it was easier to let it happen than to say no." The more I heard these comments, and over time I heard them in many high school classes, the more I thought about what students were really communicating.

The underlying issue that informed their responses was basic: my students didn't have the skills to pay attention and develop an awareness of *what was happening, in the moment, with their bodies, emotions, and thoughts.* In other words, by the time they understood what they were doing, experiencing, and/or enduring, it was too late. As a result, they had far fewer available options than they would have had before their sexual activity escalated to that stage. They couldn't say no, in part, because they had trouble accurately interpreting what was happening—much less predicting what was coming next.

Most health education models are based on the presumption that people do know what's happening and can therefore assess situations and make rational choices. Even social and emotional learning (SEL) curricula assume that students already have some basic familiarity with self-awareness and self-reflection on which to build specific competencies with practice. But what if students don't have this baseline level of awareness and the attendant option of informed behaviors?

Telling them about prevention wasn't going to help if they *weren't present while taking risks.* My immediate challenge was to teach students the skills that would enable them to "show up" and be active agents in their own lives. In short, they needed to learn *to notice what they were doing in the moment* so they could *decide what to do next*. Mindful teaching facilitated my insight, but I knew the quality of my presence by itself would not translate directly into students' skill development.

That's when I began teaching mindfulness at school.

It's been a little more than fifteen years since my initial experiences with mindfulness in the classroom. Since then, I've met many other teachers and students whose interests and work have enriched my understanding and skills. I am indebted to the teachers who nurtured me as a student and encouraged me to teach. In addition, I am immensely grateful for my family, friends, and colleagues whose input, trust, and inspiration gives me the confidence to teach as I learn, and to continue learning through teaching.

Several individuals helped bring this book into being through their incredible generosity and attention. Their gift to me, and through this book to you, reflects their love of learning and dedication to teaching. In particular, I wish to acknowledge the sage advice, as well as unbounded skill and kindness, I received at every step of the way from Josh Bartok, Senior Editor at Wisdom Publications. I am also grateful to Goldie Hawn, Gianni Faedda, and Theo Koffler who encouraged me "to do what I had to do," and whose wisdom, work, and care guided me. Heartfelt thanks to Diana Rose of the Garrison Institute for her friendship and the opportunity to work so closely together for four precious years.

Thanks to my dear friend, Sukeshi Sheth, who appeared unexpectedly at the best possible time and joined in creating this book. In addition, I am indebted to Cesar Piotto and Allison Graboski for their unwavering support, understanding, and humor; Stephen Viola, for his input and expertise; Dawn

Lamping, for her meticulous attention to detail and heartfelt enthusiasm; and Ezra Doner, for his wise counsel.

Finally, my experience writing this book ends as it began, beyond words, with my family: Joede, Mirelle, Raphael, my parents, and my brother Graham; and my teachers: A.R., R.T.R., and H.H.K.

Deborah Schoeberlein

CHAPTER 1
Teach as You Learn

"We're doing spring cleaning up here." He tapped her forehead with a long finger. "Once you put everything into its proper place—once you organize your mind—you'll be able to find what you want quickly."

Tamora Pierce, *Wild Magic*

MASTER TEACHERS ARE MINDFUL TEACHERS, aware of themselves and attuned to their students. *Mindful teaching* nurtures a learning community in which students flourish academically, emotionally, and socially—and teachers thrive professionally and personally. *Teaching mindfulness* directly to students augments the effects of the teacher's presence by coaching youth to exercise simple, practical, and universal attention skills themselves. These two approaches are mutually reinforcing and benefit everyone in the classroom.

Mindfulness is a conscious, purposeful way of tuning in to what's happening in and around us. This specific approach to paying attention and honing awareness improves mental focus and academic performance. It also strengthens skills that contribute to emotional balance. The best of our human qualities, including the capacity for kindness, empathy, and compassion, support and are supported by mindfulness. Mindfulness and deep caring contribute to healthy relationships at school and at home. Mindfulness is the means, and deep caring describes the manner.

School-based learning is complex, in part because teachers and students carry individual webs of knowledge, attitudes, skills, and behaviors into an interactive classroom environment. Learning is most effective when teachers initiate the process of weaving these varied webs together. To do so, teachers need to understand their own inner experiences, recognize their students' needs, and implement appropriate educational strategies. The teacher's own skills in attention and awareness drive this process; the stronger these skills, the better the outcomes—for everyone.

Attention and awareness are dynamic, and this means that you can sharpen them and enhance them. One of the most powerful ways to do this—for yourself and with your students—is by cultivating mindfulness. The approach involves learning and practicing some brief, simple mental training techniques and teaching methodologies. Once you learn the basics, you can bring mindfulness into your normal routine at home and at school—directly and indirectly.

This book explores two main themes that twine together to apply mindfulness to education. The first concerns the educator's direct experience of mindful teaching and the related benefits for students. The second, training students to develop mindfulness themselves, addresses the process of introducing specific techniques directly to youth at school, or more broadly, on the playing field; in the context of home-schooling; or during an after-school program, camp, or any other learning environment.

Implicit in these themes is the assumption that training attention and developing awareness of the present moment are appropriate educational activities, whether or not the term "mindfulness" is used. So, the salient question concerns methodology—how can teachers go about applying mindfulness to teaching and implementing developmentally appropriate techniques with their students?

There are multiple responses to this question, and determining which is most likely to suit your situation begins with identifying your specific context. Are you, as an individual teacher, embarking on this initiative in the classroom alone? Or are you one of many teachers, if not an entire school community, implementing mindfulness as part of a formal curriculum? In addition, will you include guest presentations, and if so, will these fill an essential or supplemental role?

The following chapters explore common issues relevant to all three of these sets of circumstances and identify significant topics pertinent to the distinct approaches. You'll also find sample strategies that promote mindful teaching and teach students about mindfulness directly. In addition, I've included a number of scripted instructions for generic mindfulness techniques that you can pick up and immediately use in the classroom. I developed some of these techniques, others are in public circulation in some form or other.

All of these formal techniques and informal activities enrich the conceptual discussion of teaching methodologies and lesson implementation. I encourage you to adopt and adapt any of them to suit your own circumstances and inclinations.

What Mindfulness Does

Mindfulness isn't a panacea for the world's problems, but it does provide a practical strategy for working directly with reality. You might not be able to change certain things in your life, at work, or at home, but you can change *how* you experience those immutable aspects of life, work, and home. And the more present you are to your own life, the more choices you have that influence its unfolding.

With mindfulness, you're more likely to view a really challenging class as just that, "a really challenging class," instead of feeling that the experience has somehow ruined your entire day. Purposefully taking a mental step back, in order to notice what happened without immediately engaging with intense emotions and reactions, provides a kind of protection against unconstructive responses and the self-criticism that can slip out and make a hard thing even harder. Even just pausing to take a breath can help you slow down, see a broader perspective and redirect the energy of the situation.

I've had moments (as I'm sure have you) when a cascade of little annoyances gathered momentum and I lost it—only to regret my outburst later. Developing mindfulness promotes awareness of the cascade, but from a distance. This way, I have a better chance of working with my assumptions without losing my perspective. Annoyances can be events that don't have to gain momentum, rather than triggers for more and more difficulty. Mindfully noticing the discrepancy between what *I wanted to accomplish* and what *I actually achieved* provides useful information without the distraction of unproductive anger, frustration, or disappointment.

I've also known days when one challenging class rattled me to my core and poisoned whatever came next. Even after school, such experiences often lingered—as if the actual class weren't bad enough, the ongoing mental repercussions were worse. If this has happened to you, then you'll know exactly how painful and frustrating this feels. It's easy to torment yourself by questioning your competence as a teacher when a forty-five minute class can cause you to take students' poor behavior personally and lose your center. Even reflecting, "I should have handled that differently since I'm a professional after all—and I'm the adult in a room full of kids!" doesn't really provide any practical guidance for the future.

So what's the answer? Put simply, part of it is all about mindfulness: practice and application, and more practice and yet more application. Practice begins with developing mindfulness in a calm, quiet place, a place where the practice is comparatively easy. Application is about walking into a more challenging situation in real life, like your most difficult class, with increased skills and the confidence to help you stay focused, present, flexible, and available. Should you lose the quality of mindfulness you'll eventually notice what's happened. And when you do, you can practice returning your attention to paying attention, and redirect your awareness onto the experience of awareness. As you practice and apply mindfulness, you'll gain skills that will help you accurately assess challenges and handle them with greater ease.

Having techniques that help you manage your own experiences and emotions is more comfortable than feeling powerless as a result of your emotions and habits or, worse, buffeted about by the changing winds of other people's behaviors and the environment. It's a simple fact of life that we cannot change other people to suit our will. Yet you can change your own habits and your relationship to your reactions—but reaching that goal requires effective strategies.

Learning mindfulness techniques that support *responding* rather than *reacting* allows you to align your emotional patterns and your actions with your current understanding and needs.

Mindful Teaching: You've Done It Before

Most likely, you've already experienced moments of mindfulness, but perhaps not recognized them as such at the time— or at least not until afterward. Even if you haven't, the techniques in this book will help you develop that awareness. Considering these examples might prompt the recollection of similar experiences:

- You're teaching a class when you notice—as if you were witnessing the situation while living it—your students and you are totally focused on the experience of learning.
- You're listening to someone when you realize you're totally tuned in to the experience of listening—and you're not thinking at all about what to say next.
- You consciously hear your tone of voice while speaking and notice how sounds can communicate—without automatically focusing on the meaning of the words.

These are all examples of becoming aware of mindfulness. That realization of "Ooh! I'm being really mindful of this moment!" is not itself the experience of mindfulness. When you're truly present in the moment, your awareness isn't split between your experience of presence and your commentary about the experience. Mindfulness precedes the recognition of self-awareness, and the commentary may or may not arise afterward.

Another way to identify mindfulness is by examining mind-*less*ness—the quality of losing your awareness of what's happening inside and around you. See if you recognize any of these examples from your own experience:

- You react very strongly to a relatively minor issue with a student, and later realize your emotional arousal was due to something else, and had nothing to do with what happened in class.
- You suddenly notice a colleague has been speaking to you for at least fifteen minutes and you've missed most (all?) of what she said.
- You gulp down your lunch only to realize you didn't taste a bite.

Most teachers intuitively know the feeling of being in or out of sync with themselves as well as their students. Or, to put it differently, you probably feel the qualitative difference between mindful and mindless teaching. When you're *really here*, your teaching is effective and you feel energized. In contrast, mindless teaching isn't so effective, and often leads to feeling drained and cranky.

There is also a noticeable difference in students' performance when they learn mindfully versus when they do schoolwork mindlessly. When students are *really there*, the classroom is alive with learning and their work shines. When they're disengaged or distracted, well, the classroom is more likely to be dull or in chaos.

Mind and Brain

Using the mind to know the mind is a uniquely human capacity, as is using the mind to change the brain and thus the body. In this book, I use the term *mind* to refer to consciousness and the term *brain* for the organ, located within the skull, that supports consciousness. This is not a strictly scientific distinction, but differentiating between the mind and brain simplifies the discussion considerably.

My high school biology teachers taught that the human brain stops growing after adolescence. My classmates and I didn't welcome this information. We resisted the idea that our brain's power would begin to wane once we reached adulthood. Contemporary high school students learn that the connections among the 100+ billion neurons in the brain are "plastic," and can change throughout a lifetime. Today's students might take this information for granted, but knowing it's not all downhill after age 21 helps motivate me to make the effort required to train my mind during adulthood.

Old dogs *can* learn new tricks. Regular mindfulness practice trains attention, promotes emotional balance, fosters a sense of well-being, and thus leads to physiological and anatomical changes in the brain associated with these experiences. Other changes in the body demonstrate further benefits of ongoing mindfulness practice, including heightened immunity, improved stress-management skills, and reduced exposure to stress hormones. These health-related outcomes are relevant at school, since good health makes teaching easier and more effective. It also promotes learning and successful performance in both students and teachers.

BENEFITS OF MINDFULNESS

FOR TEACHERS:

- Improves focus and awareness.
- Increases responsiveness to students' needs.
- Promotes emotional balance.
- Supports stress management and stress reduction.
- Supports healthy relationships at work and home.
- Enhances classroom climate.
- Supports overall well-being.

FOR STUDENTS:

- Supports "readiness to learn."
- Promotes academic performance.
- Strengthens attention and concentration.
- Reduces anxiety before testing.
- Promotes self-reflection and self-calming.
- Improves classroom participation by supporting impulse control.
- Provides tools to reduce stress.
- Enhances social and emotional learning.
- Fosters pro-social behaviors and healthy relationships.
- Supports holistic well-being.

Taking Mindfulness to School

The most common model for taking mindfulness to school relies on an individual teacher—perhaps someone like you—with an interest in the subject. Perhaps you stumbled on a reference to mindfulness while searching for strategies that help students concentrate on their work or calm their minds more effectively. Or maybe you have personal experience with mindfulness and wonder whether this practice could help your students—and, if so, how to teach it to them.

Most teachers start bringing mindfulness to school without the benefit of professional training on the subject. That's fine and can be effective, but first it's important to gain familiarity with the experience of mindfulness on your own. As you do so, you'll naturally bring your heightened attention and awareness into the classroom and teach more mindfully.

This type of personal development supports professional development, and you don't need administrative approval for mindful teaching so long as the outcomes are consistent with standard practice. Everyone accepts that patience, attentiveness, and responsiveness are desirable, even essential, qualities for teachers. How you cultivate them is secondary as long as you maintain a professional presence at school.

There are other approaches and considerations if you want to teach mindfulness more directly to your students than simply through your own informal modeling. The most comprehensive approach is to use a formal mindfulness curriculum—which might not be practical given the specifics of your class, school, or situation. One potential difficulty with this strategy lies in the paucity of curricula and training programs accessible to individual teachers. Typically, formal curricula are only available to schools and school districts for pedagogical as well as practical reasons such as financial cost. As an individual teacher, you're also likely to face obstacles related to obtaining administrative approval for a new curriculum, especially when other teachers are satisfied with existing materials.

Fortunately, there are other options better suited for use by an individual teacher. The most promising of these is to integrate discrete and simple mindfulness techniques within your existing curricula or regular schedule. In addition to developing your own familiarity with mindfulness, you'll also need to find developmentally appropriate techniques for your students or develop them yourself (and this book will set you well on your way to doing this). You can easily introduce short techniques during class, homeroom, or even during the few minutes left before or after you mark attendance, go to lunch, or dismiss your students. More elaborate and time-intensive activities are less flexible, but you can still introduce them as lesson extensions or during special events. Whether you'll need administrative approval for this type of curricular enhancement is likely to depend on your chosen approach, school policy, and community norms.

Peer support is important—for teachers and students—and teaching mindfulness is easier, and arguably more effective, in schools and school districts where everyone participates. Getting everyone involved in a schoolwide program that incorporates research-based methodologies requires strong administrative support—but schools are also more likely to approve large-scale, demonstrated methodologies. Once adopted, such programs have the greatest potential to impact the overall school culture as well as individual classroom climate.

From the teacher's perspective, there are other, more immediate, benefits associated with using an approved mindfulness curriculum. Generally, approved curricula are comprehensive and include developmentally appropriate lesson plans with performance measures for students, background information for teachers, and cross-references aligning curricular content with education standard for administrators. All these components facilitate planning, implementation, and evaluation.

Formal curricula typically include a teacher-training component. At a minimum, the training covers the nuts-and-bolts aspects of implementation, addressing issues like *how* to present each lesson and *when* to assess whether students are learning. Enhanced training goes further by presenting new curricular content to teachers, providing them with instruction in new skills, and offering opportunities for supervised practice and feedback. While direct interaction with an official trainer is standard practice, other promising options include instructional DVDs and online education, both of which are less expensive and time-intensive.

The third model for bringing mindfulness to school minimizes, if not eliminates, the need for teacher training since guest presenters carry the responsibility for presenting the material. Enhancing classroom-based mindfulness instruction by exposing students to a credible resource from outside the school community is a common, and often very productive, strategy for involving guest presenters. This methodology works best when you prepare students in advance and introduce the presenter in the context of ongoing study, and follow-up later to reinforce their learning.

Another approach involves community-based presenters with a contractual relationship to provide regular school-based instruction in specific subject areas, such as yoga, Tai Chi, or meditation. These guest presenters have special expertise, and fill in for regular teachers with full administrative support.

Yet another option is inviting guest presenters to school for a one-time-only event. As a stand-alone approach, this model has limited long-term impact—it's difficult to develop mindfulness or understand a basic mindfulness practice within the course of a single lecture. Nonetheless, a special event can work beautifully if classroom teachers support students' practice afterward and provide reinforcement as the students develop new skills.

The classroom teacher's role is critical to the success of any approach that takes mindfulness to school. Your presence will inform your students' experience regardless of whether you take the lead in developing techniques, implementing a curriculum or bringing in a guest presenter. Mindful teaching supports teaching mindfulness.

While you don't need to have extensive prior experience, the familiarity that comes with a little practice does help by building the confidence needed for teaching mindfulness effectively in the classroom.

Personal Practice: Beginning Now

Gaining experience with mindfulness sets you up to teach authentically within your comfort zone. There's a huge difference between teaching something "I think ought to be useful" and something "I know, from my own experience, is useful." You don't need to have significant *expertise*—rather, you just need to practice yourself so you have an *experiential foundation* on which to base your teaching.

The learning sequence for mindfulness is essentially the same one you already use when you teach students other skills, from math to music, or language arts to athletics. Information and instruction come first followed by lots of practice. Over time, the brain becomes familiar with generating mindfulness. With repetition, these skills become more automatic and require less effort.

In the beginning, a few minutes to practice mindfulness can feel like an eternity, so using short sessions is appropriate. Then, as you become more accustomed to the techniques, you might choose to practice longer. It's good to go at your own speed and see what happens. And just five minutes practice regularly is more useful in the long-run than longer sessions done more sporadically. All you need to do to get started is "Take 5."

Begin by taking five minutes to sit still, by yourself, in a quiet, comfortable, and private place. Turn off the ringers of your phones, turn off the TV or radio, and put aside your "to-do" list. If you're concerned about how long you're going to practice, set a timer that has an audible bell or flashing light.

It's best to sit in a stable position, with your spine as straight as possible, either on a chair without leaning against the back, or cross-legged on a comfortable cushion set on the floor. Place both your hands in your lap or palm-down on your thighs. The idea is to get comfortable without getting caught up in trying to find a position of perfect comfort. And, of course, don't sit in a way that causes you serious pain—or lulls you to sleep.

Once you're settled, allow your gaze to soften and gently go out of focus as you keep your eyes slightly open. Look forward and downward at a 45°angle so that your eyelids relax and lower a little. Try to breathe through your nose, and let your lips, mouth, and jaw relax. Now that you're in position, you can begin the basic breathing practice outlined in the following progression.

TAKE 5: MINDFUL BREATHING (FOR TEACHERS)

- Breathe normally, paying attention to the feeling of the breath as it fills your lungs and then flows up and back out the way it came.
- Notice when you lose awareness of the breath and

start thinking about something else, daydreaming, worrying, or snoozing.

- Return your attention to the breath, with kindness toward yourself and as little commentary as possible.

When you first begin mindfulness practice, you're likely to pay attention to the breath for a few seconds and then lose focus. That's perfectly natural! You'll eventually become aware that the focus of your attention moved away from the breath and onto something else. You might feel like you're becoming even more mindless. All these sensations are normal, and in fact, they signify that the practice is working—you're noticing what's really happening. If thoughts about the quality of your practice come (because that's what thoughts do…), don't worry about them, just notice them and refocus on watching what's happening right now.

The essence of this technique is attending to the process (the experience of noticing) without getting caught up in content (what the thoughts are about). First, simply notice thoughts as they first appear on the horizon of your mind. Keep some distance as you watch them and let them fade away. This is the difference between witnessing thoughts and engaging with them. It's an attitude of, "Oh, here are some thoughts about work (or a relationship or something else), but I'm not going to get into them now." Be gentle with yourself, and patient, and kind.

As you practice mindfulness, you might start noticing all sorts of changes in your daily life. You might be less reactive, and more likely to pause and breathe when something comes up. You might also notice that pausing for breath facilitates your ability to choose a response that promotes better outcomes for everyone. Amid all of this, you might begin to take pleasure, or find more pleasure, in your mindfulness practice and seek new opportunities during the day in which to Take 5. In addition, you might also notice greater patience and kindness in relationship with your sense of self.

Cultivating mindfulness begins with practicing a simple progression like Mindful Breathing and becoming adept at moving through the three basic phases: (1) committing to practice and doing so; (2) noticing your breath and remembering that you're noticing it; and (3) refocusing and returning to parctice when you become distracted. Then, as mindfulness becomes more familiar, you'll focus your attention and extend your awareness more spontaneously while you gain the experience that supports teaching the practice to others.

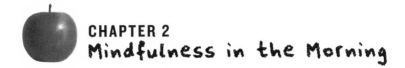

CHAPTER 2
Mindfulness in the Morning

[Sherlock] Holmes had cultivated the ability to still
the noise of the mind....
                    Laurie R. King, *The Beekeeper's Apprentice*

MINDFULNESS INSTILLS freshness as you move through the
morning. Noticing what you're doing *as* you're doing it initiates the transformation. Even if you're not a morning person,
there is no need for radical change. As you'll see, there are
many simple strategies that can help you shift the experiential
quality of your normal routine by focusing attention and
awareness on *how* you do what you do.

The very first opportunity for mindfulness occurs as you
transition from sleep into wakefulness. If you bring mindful
attention to the process of waking, you may start to find that
the quality and texture of your day differs from simply moving automatically through your morning routine.

The objective in waking mindfully is paying attention,
deeply, regardless of whether your immediate experience is
marked by calm or chaos.

Greeting the Day

What's the first thing you like to do when your students enter the classroom? I like to greet them by acknowledging their presence and communicating welcome. This feels good for me, and I know they are more likely to learn when they soften into the learning environment. Since genuine greetings support positive outcomes in the classroom, why not adapt the same methodology first thing in the morning?

Best practices in the classroom are often relevant at home. I like to acknowledge the experience of shifting from sleep into conscious awareness silently, with a sense of gratitude. The feeling is more an attitude than a statement, but it includes recognition—"I'm here, now"—and appreciation—"I'm glad to know that I'm here."

You might greet the day silently, or with words like "Here I am," "Okay, it's morning. Let's go," or "Hello, day!" Or you might look out the window each morning before you get out of bed to meet the day with your eyes. The nature of a greeting is personal; it has to feel right for you as both giver and receiver.

Mindfulness plays a role in all these greetings. First, you attend to the experience of noticing that it's morning. Next, you begin to become aware that your experience of noticing the morning cues you to greet the day. Finally, you offer your greeting with awareness that this greeting welcomes you to the day and the day to you. Greeting the day involves witnessing and participating in its arrival, and your gesture of acknowledgment merges mindfulness with your behavior.

Mindfulness and Intentions

Setting an intention that highlights an aspect of daily experience builds on your initial greeting. Developing an intention is similar to visualizing, but instead of a picture you develop a mental, emotional, or *attitudinal* model of what you would like to accomplish or perhaps just the *way* you intend to encounter activities.

"Casting an intention" over the day is like throwing a ship's anchor into the sea. Once the anchor is lodged in the sea floor, the ship maintains its general location even if the wind and tides alter its surface position. Likewise, an intention positions your mind to hold a particular orientation during the day, as you shift between activities. Mindfulness is the line that attaches the anchor of intention with your moment-by-moment experiences during the day.

Intentions and mindfulness reinforce each other. Intention focuses attention on a particular objective, and mindfulness harnesses awareness to sustain your focus.

Mindfulness permeates the process of working with an intention at multiple points:

- When you *set* the intention, and think, "I aspire to express more patience today when I work with (a specified class, student, or other situation)."
- When you *notice* your experience through the day while recalling your intention, and say, "Here I am working with (whomever or whatever you specified), and I'm acting impatiently."
- When you *return* to your intention, with the thought, "Remember, now is the time to practice patience...patience...patience."

- When you consciously *do something* to support or embody your intention, and think, "Here I am choosing to express and embody patience, even though I could have been feeling really frustrated," or "Okay, I'm feeling frustrated, and it's time to take a slow breath and practice patience."
- When you *acknowledge* later that you did something aligned with your intention without consciously thinking about it, such as, "I was really able to be patient with that student's acting up in class today—a few months ago I probably would have lost it!"

Since intentions are powerful, it's important to have and reinforce realistic and constructive mental models of what you want to do or how you want to respond. Setting an intention primes you to embody a certain quality. It improves your sensitivity so that you are more likely to notice opportunities and make the effort to actualize your intention.

Conversely, repeatedly reviewing how things could go wrong focuses attention unconstructively. Athletics provides a helpful example. A skier heading down the mountain in a forest needs to look at the spaces between the trees (where she wants to go) rather than the trees themselves (lest she hit them). In the context of school, the intention to breathe before speaking during a tense faculty meeting builds confidence, whereas focusing on your nervousness can trigger the jitters.

Intentions can encompass behaviors, attitudes, thoughts, and feelings and it's best to work with them one at a time, day by day. Aside from scale, they are similar in many ways to New Year's resolutions, and they also provoke the temptation to make magnificent changes (such as lose thirty pounds, stop smoking, act more kindly with the in-laws, or stop yelling at challenging students). The sheer magnitude of these goals often draws attention away from the practical issues concerning the process of realizing them.

As a result, it's easy to aim for a splendid outcome only to find that your resolution sets you up for frustration and (if you conclude by giving up) failure. Sure, it might be wonderful to lose thirty pounds by the end of the year, but weight loss is an every-day activity and what you do today poses the more practical measure of success. Despite the temptation to look toward the finish line, common sense confirms that working with bite-sized intentions and making progress incrementally feels and works better.

I learned this the hard way. When I first explored setting intentions, I immediately set lofty goals such as to "stay patient with everyone, all day" and to "refrain from feeling angry about anything ever." Perhaps unsurprisingly, I forgot most of these lofty first intentions almost as quickly as I made them. When I did manage to remember them in the midst of a trying day, my objectives appeared so unrealistic as to be unreachable, and therefore, irrelevant to me in any given moment. Eventually, I learned to change my approach, setting more modest and achievable intentions—and, as a result, meeting my goals more and more often. Much later, as my skills and confidence grew, I was able to increase the scope of my aspiration in reasonable increments.

Behavioral intentions provide a constructive starting point because they are often the most obvious objectives. For example, after greeting the day, you could set the intention to eat breakfast slowly and carefully chew at least *some* bites, *on this particular morning.*

Discrete intentions offer reasonable odds of success because they prompt simple alterations to familiar activities that occur shortly after you wake up. Both the relatively small adjustment in the activity and the brief interval between planning and actualizing the intention support success. While you can work with the same intention repeatedly, its may be productive to switch to a new objective after several days, and then return to the original intention when doing so feels fresh again.

As you gain familiarity with setting intentions, you'll naturally begin to focus on objectives that require a little more effort—either because the tasks are more demanding or they occur later in the day. A simple way to increase the challenge is to set intentions specific to being at school where there are greater distractions than at home.

Intentions at School

There are many possible foci for behavioral intentions at school. Focusing on the quality of your personal experience on just one day, today, is a good place to start since you have more control over what you do than over what happens around you. Begin with something very tangible, like carrying less weight in your bag or getting up to stretch before you grade papers during your planning period. If you've felt exhausted from the constant demands of students over the past weeks, set an intention to close your door and take a few *moments* to practice mindful breathing *today at noon*.

General directives concerning emotions and attitudes, such as "take time to rest" or "stay calm," are difficult to implement, even within a specified context. It's easier to give yourself the benefit of supporting details concerning "how" to fulfill an intention, rather than "where" or "when." So, instead of planning to "be patient" during a potentially explosive meeting, set the intention to notice when your body tenses with stress (maybe your jaw clenches or your neck tightens or you hear a rush of blood in your ears) and when you do notice, to then pause and take a breath. You could even write yourself a reminder to help you remember your plan.

Intentions can also promote qualities or feelings that support healthy self-esteem for others and yourself. If, for instance, you want to give more positive attention to your most challenging students, you could develop the intention to find an opportunity to offer sincere praise to one of them during a specific class today, even if the praise simply acknowledges attendance.

There are days when I feel overwhelmed and exhausted by challenges and difficulties, so much so that I forget to notice pleasant events or gestures of kindness. The momentum takes hold and its hard to separate discrete moments from the blur. If you've had similar experiences, you could try the strategy that worked for me.

Begin by setting the intention to notice and relish something nice before you leave home in the morning—just one thing. The next day, set the same intention but shift the timing so you notice something nice during your first class of the day—try to notice something at the beginning of class one day, the end of class another, and in the middle on a third. Every day, change the timing or the number of nice events. Training your mind to notice and acknowledge noticing these pleasant experiences can increase your awareness of their presence. As a consequence of following through on even this simple intention, you may well find your day starts to feel just a little nicer, even if the total number of individual unpleasant experiences remains constant.

Working with specific intentions is constructive even under the most trying circumstances, especially if you've practiced the technique under easier conditions. Imagine you are lying in bed, having greeted the day rather unenthusiastically because you woke up dreaming about last month's staff meeting, at which you learned that your school is closing permanently at the end of this year. As you look back over the past weeks, you realize each day you've spent in the classroom has left you more short-tempered, anxious, and preoccupied.

You recognize you've got to manage your intense, albeit normal and perfectly understandable, emotions so you can find solace in completing the school year as gracefully as possible. Although getting through this transition will likely require the support of friends and family, and possibly the guidance and advice of colleagues and other professionals, you can initiate productive changes today.

It's time to set an intention. While you may be tempted to set a broad intention to "ignore your emotions and teach well today," you realize you have to formulate a specific plan to help you through the day. You're already familiar with the sequence of setting an intention, followed by remembering and actualizing it. Apply these steps by forming and holding the goal to notice your feelings, as they arise, and gently put them to the side of your awareness until later in the day.

Each time your attention shifts to ride a wave of intense emotion, you can pause to breathe and mentally nod acknowledgment to the feeling even as you direct your focus back to the intention. You can then resolve later to attend in depth to the content of your reactions and feelings. The point is to focus on increasing recognition of your emotions without permitting them to carry you away. The intention is to apply this mental gesture of awareness, as often as necessary, so you deal directly with your emotions without sabotaging your class-room responsibilities. After school, remember to complete the intention by giving yourself permission to attend to your feelings as planned.

The Objective Isn't the Only Goal

Although intentions are linked to specific objectives, their deeper value lies in providing a method for purposefully cultivating awareness. Don't worry if "today is too busy" to fulfill your intention about, for instance, a non-working lunch. The most important part is noticing what's actually happening, in the moment.

This is why the process of working with intentions is ultimately more important than *whether or not you actually fulfill them*. Intentions provide a useful format for practicing basic skills. This is analogous to focusing your math students on manipulating examples of specific patterns so they develop fluency with the skills that enable them to apply the same processes to patterns in general.

The experience of setting and then holding an intention is not necessarily comfortable. You might meet resistance and find endless reasons to postpone fulfilling your plan. If you intended to sit down for a non-working lunch, your mind might try to convince you, "it's a nice intention, but today is too busy, so why not try it again tomorrow." Such comments emerge frequently as intentions challenge habitual patterns.

Although it's easy to view these inner comments as pesky annoyances, they are simply expressions of ideas to which you've grown accustomed. They are much like the thoughts that come and go during mindful breathing. Once you recognize your mind's arguments as thoughts, you can let them dissipate. Be kind to yourself, and give yourself credit even for just remembering to form or return to your intention. Wholesome feelings increase the motivation to continue expending the effort necessary for personal growth.

Setting an intention, like greeting the day, doesn't need to take a long time. When bolstered by attention and awareness, however, the effects can last throughout the day. This means, in addition to setting an intention, it is also important to make the time to practice mindfulness regularly so that you develop the stamina and skill required to sustain attention.

Take 5 for a Month

Greeting the day provides a framework for taking five minutes to practice mindful breathing, which in turn supports working with an intention throughout the day. Just as dancers warm up with routine exercises before performing a choreographed piece, taking five minutes for mindful breathing prepares you to apply mindfulness to daily experience.

Try making a deal with yourself: you'll take five minutes every school day morning for one month to practice mindful breathing. That's just twenty-five minutes in a week—and you get weekends off! Doing this on weekdays gives you the most direct opportunity to extend your heightened awareness of mindfulness beyond your five-minute practice session into your professional activities.

At the end of the month, you can assess the preliminary results of your own mindfulness experiment. If you feel a positive difference overall, then you'll feel more confident of the benefits of practice. Your personal results will also help bolster your enthusiasm for the practice and motivation to continue.

If, on the other hand, you don't feel the practice helped

you, you'll have the confidence that comes from having tried it for yourself and learned from the outcomes and made an informed decision. Formal mindfulness practice might not be the best fit for you. If that's so, it is tremendously important to honor your instincts and explore other strategies that can lead to mental awareness and emotional balance.

Mindfulness of Thoughts and Emotions

Focusing mindfulness on noticing thoughts, and later on noticing emotions, is the logical next step after you gain basic familiarity with mindful breathing. In order to take this step, you can adapt the core progression from Take 5. As you'll see in the instructions below, the adaptation is more a shift in emphasis, rather than a change in approach.

NOTICING THOUGHTS: A VARIATION ON TAKE 5 (FOR TEACHERS)

- Breathe normally, paying attention to the feeling of the breath as it fills your lungs and then flows up and back out the way it came.
- Notice when a thought (a mental event that involves words) arises.
- Acknowledge the thought by saying "thinking" or "ah yes, a thought" silently in your mind.
- Switch your attention from that thought in particular, back to watching for thoughts in general.
- Continue watching thoughts and acknowledging them inwardly until your session ends.
- As always, be patient, gentle, and kind with yourself.

In Take 5, the point is to notice thoughts, feelings, and other sensations and then refocus on the breath. In this variation, you still notice thoughts, but do so more purposefully and label these mental events as *thoughts*. Doing so allows you to notice them "generically" without delving into their content. In effect, you're acknowledging that "thoughts are just thoughts" and not themselves ironclad directives for action or even ultimate truths. They come and go because that's what thoughts do. You can attend to them or not, because that's also what the mind does.

The same holds true for feelings. However, whereas thoughts involve words, feelings are the directly *felt* experience of emotions. In this case, "feelings" refer to emotional experiences including reactions, not physical or "felt" sensations such as heat, cold, or pain. You can adapt Take 5 to focus on developing mindfulness of your feelings like this:

NOTICING FEELINGS: A VARIATION ON TAKE 5 (FOR TEACHERS)

- Breathe normally, paying attention to the feeling of the breath as it fills your lungs and then flows up and back out the way it came.
- Notice when a feeling or emotional reaction arises.
- Acknowledge the feeling by saying "feeling" or "ah yes, a reaction" silently in your mind.
- Switch your attention from that feeling in particular, back to watching for emotions in general.
- Continue watching emotions and saying "feeling" until your session ends.
- As always, be patient, gentle, and kind with yourself.

As with developing mindfulness of thoughts, the idea is to notice and feel emotions without specifying what type. The technique involves just acknowledging the *fact* of feeling or reaction. There's no need to reinforce the internal story by elaborating on details; so for instance rather than describing "feeling bored," "feeling uneasy," or "feeling peaceful," you would just acknowledge all of them as belonging to the category of "feeling." With practice, you'll increase your ability to recognize the presence of emotion without immediately getting pulled into it or automatically acting on it. This is useful because mindfulness of emotions increases conscious awareness of them, and enhances our ability to manage them at will.

If you're already practicing Take 5, try extending your sessions by adding either of these variations after you spend some time simply focusing on mindful breathing. Beginning with the breath calms your mind and centers your attention as a lead-in to other mindfulness practices. Then you can use the rhythm of the breath as the backdrop for shifting to a different object of attention.

The basic sequence common among these variations builds on the steps to mindful breathing with which you are already familiar. First you watch as thoughts and emotions arise. Then you acknowledge the mind's recognition of them by saying "thinking" or "feeling." The third step involves watching as they disperse as well as noticing when new ones arise. If they linger, you can acknowledge them again (and again), until they drift away—even if only to return again and offer you more opportunity to practice with them.

When the same thoughts and feelings persist, or new ones seem to arise continuously without interruption, you might spend the entire practice time silently acknowledging the activity in your mind. That's fine. In fact, it's a good sign—

you're simply noticing what's happening as it's happening. The opposite experience can also arise—you might realize you hardly notice any distinct thoughts or emotions although you are aware of watching for them. That's fine, too.

The quality of paying attention is the main attraction, whether you have lots of mental activity or hardly any at all. The level of activity is dynamic, and will change day by day. There's no need to privilege the experience of having fewer thoughts and feelings over more of them. A low level of mental activity doesn't necessarily indicate whether you are more or less mindful—you could truly be aware of a temporarily calm mind, or you could be distracted to the point where you "spaced out" on noticing your thoughts and emotions. And an experience of a quiet mind or peacefulness doesn't in itself indicate mindfulness. Some periods are calm and quiet, others are busy and agitated. The specifics of what's actually happening are less important than cultivating a steady, alert experience of noticing.

Anchoring the Day

The process of developing mindfulness requires time, both for daily practice and for slow, organic growth over the course of years. It's important to work with this type of meditation in moderation, so find the commitment level manageable for you. It's a simple fact of our modern lives that sometimes we have to multitask. This means you'll need to pick and choose where and when to practice mindfulness intentionally.

Morning activities are typically discrete, so they provide ideal opportunities to exercise mindfulness. As you consider the options, keep in mind you'll want to select among them— maybe one a day, each day—until the practice requires perhaps just a little less effort. As you do this, you're likely to notice you experience mindfulness spontaneously at other times. As your mindfulness becomes more stable and sustainable, it will also seem increasingly normal and gradually permeate more and more of your day.

For now, consider the obvious options for experiencing different aspects of your morning routine as mini mindfulness activities. For example, mindful brushing of your teeth asks you to focus all your attention on that experience. Simple as this sounds, it's rather challenging. You might normally open the window shade or go to the kitchen to turn on the kettle or coffee pot while brushing. Instead, stay by the sink and feel the sensation of the brush in your mouth, listen to the sound of the brushing, notice the feel of the toothpaste on your tongue. Notice the way your arm and hand move as you brush. Then attend to the feeling of the water when you rinse your mouth as you finish caring for your teeth before moving on to the next activity.

Or, when you get dressed, bring mindfulness to the experience of choosing your clothes. Place your awareness on color, texture, and shape. Then explore the visual and tactile experience of putting each garment on. Attend to each movement as you clothe your body, whether you do it quickly or very slowly.

Another option is to have a little fun while trying to "match" your clothes to your intention for the day. Do you wear a certain color that corresponds with your mood or schedule? Or do the patterns on your neckties or scarves provide clues that prompt your students to predict the lesson of the day? Consider what you see when you look at yourself in the mirror—do you see colors, shapes, textures, or specific items like shirts, skirts, or pants? Or do you compare your reflection with an image in your mind and launch an inner narrative about the comparison? Mindfulness involves allowing your thoughts, feelings, and sensations to come and go as they will, not forcefully stopping them or trying not to think.

When you become aware of unconstructive thoughts or feelings that arise unexpectedly, or habitually, apply mindfulness to acknowledge them and then shift your attention to whatever you're doing, in that moment. Perhaps you really enjoy drinking sweet coffee or tea until you think about counting calories. Notice the calorie counting and then shift your attention to the texture, temperature, and taste of your beverage. Just enjoy the richness of the direct experience, whether the coffee is delicious, strong, and pungent, or you realize that the milk has turned sour and now tastes disgusting.

You might also focus on noticing the transition from thirst to contentment. Do you feel a burst of energy after drinking a smoothie or juice? Or does caffeine make you more alert? Once you notice how you experience hydrating your body, expand your focus to the experience of nourishing your body with food.

Whether or not you set a specific intention about breakfast, you can attend mindfully to the first meal of the day. Begin by considering whether you normally notice the process of preparing and eating your food, or whether you do so while reading the newspaper, watching the news, or getting your family ready for the day? When you have time, engage in mindful eating, concentrating on experiencing the taste, color, and consistency of every bite. Even when you have to rush through breakfast, notice the details and texture of that experience too.

As you prepare to leave for work, notice how your body, mind, and emotions feel. Are you calm and relaxed, or pressed for time and stressed about organizing everything you need? If you live with other people, take a moment to reflect on your interactions. Were they fulfilling or unsettling? If you notice escalating emotions and recognize the possibility of impending conflict, apply mindfulness and pause. Giving your loved ones your full attention as you say goodbye and wish them a good day is a great gift—for them and for you. Doing so helps you leave the house both physically and mentally.

Applying mindfulness to your morning gets easier over time. At first, just focus on increasing your attention during one or two specific activities while moving through the others normally. Also, remember that mindfulness is not a function of speed; and "mindful" does not itself mean "slow." As much as possible, maintain a sense of humor and perspective in the process—whatever happens.

As you work with the practice, mindfulness will become familiar. You may start to feel just a little more resilient. And the ups and downs may not take you on quite such a ride. Remember that noticing when you're gulping your food or tearing out of the house running late is as valuable as relishing a hot shower or noticing the quality of the sunshine streaming through the window.

Either way, you're paying attention and present to the day.

CHAPTER 3
On to School

Other knights of King Arthur's court were always riding out on quests—very intent on going to particular places to perform particular tasks—but Dinadan had come to accept that he was not like that. For him, it was enough to go, without necessarily arriving anywhere.

Gerald Morris, *The Ballad of Sir Dinadan*

TEACHERS MAKE THE TRANSITION from personal time to teaching somewhere between home and school, and the nature of the shift varies among individuals. The way you segue between your personal and professional responsibilities matters both in terms of the quality of your actual experience and its influence on what follows. Although commuting is unavoidable, the physical reality of moving from home to school provides a mental benefit—it creates a distinct opportunity for attending to the quality of your immediate experience.

Begin by setting an intention to focus on the quality of your commute, today. This means bringing mindfulness to the process so you notice your inner thoughts, emotions, and body sensations as well as your outer circumstances. At first, just take some time to gather information about your "normal" experience while commuting. Where do you place your attention on the way to school? Perhaps you notice the people around you, the weather, how your body feels as it moves (or sits still) and listens to morning sounds. Or maybe you focus on reading your newspaper or listening to music or news. (An important caution, however: If you are *driving* to work, it's best just to let driving be your main focus of attention; don't try to do anything else as you drive.)

Your physical environment deserves notice as well. How do you travel to school? Do you sit in a car or on a bus, or do you walk on the street? Where are you mentally as your body moves? Are you daydreaming or imagining yourself in a class that hasn't even begun? As you pay attention to what's happening around you, you're likely to become curious about the experience of commuting. Try focusing on seeing familiar sights with fresh eyes or attending to sounds as sensations without immediately attaching meanings. Explore listening to "a really loud ringing and honking" in the distance without automatically wondering, "Where's that fire truck heading?"

The act of noticing how your outer environment connects with your inner awareness is a core element of cultivating mindfulness on the way to school. One illuminating approach is to focus on how you typically respond to events beyond your control such as a car accident that stops traffic and threatens to make you late to school. Do you notice what's happening while remaining calm? Or do you register that your body, emotions, and thoughts are racing in high gear? What happens when you consider that there's nothing you can do to make the traffic move faster?

As you become familiar with applying mindfulness to the

moment, you start to have the option to work with current circumstances more skillfully. This means although you can't clear the accident, you can shift your focus from "doing something about it" to "doing something for yourself" such as breathing mindfully. Managing your emotions and calming your mind while waiting for traffic to move won't get you to school any faster, but you'll be in better shape when you do get there. Investing energy in practicing mindfulness on your way to school has significant practical value—your state of mind will influence your students' states of mind as well as your own experience of the day.

Do as I Do

Modeling is a powerful teaching strategy. If you're calm, your students will instinctively move toward their own sense of calm. If you're nervous, they will follow suit there as well. If you treat them with respect and integrity, they're likely to return the courtesy to you. This reciprocity and attunement with students supports their development and contributes to social and emotional learning (SEL).

Promoting SEL involves teaching students to develop and demonstrate skills in five main competencies: self-awareness, self-management, social awareness, relationship skills, and responsible decision-making. An effective SEL curriculum fosters academic learning and healthy behavior, as well as dynamic, safe, and responsive classrooms. Curricula are important, and often essential for classroom-based learning—yet having a teacher who can *model* SEL competencies while successfully implementing an acceptable curriculum may be equally, if not more, important.

Setting an intention to model SEL competencies is a good

place to begin, and working with self-awareness is the first step. Begin by examining what you're doing when your class is focused and calm—assuming that's the goal. Next, prompt yourself to notice what's happening when the class is not as focused or calm. Then cultivate self-awareness when things aren't going as planned and your class is distracted and acting wildly. Apply mindfulness to your thoughts and feelings so you can notice your response. Are you thinking angry thoughts that cause you to feel anxious or overwhelmed? Or are you feeling steady and confident? See what you do, and don't do, when you're in different situations.

Intense and unmanageable emotions interfere physiologically with learning (and presumably teaching) by contributing to a situation in the brain where "all circuits are busy." As a result, the system starts to shut down—and teachable moments are lost. Stress causes the brain to focus on "survival" (or its modern analogue) while ignoring everything else, including any quality study of math or language arts or steady and calm classroom management. Moreover, the aftereffects can be uncomfortable and exhausting.

Since stress is unavoidable, the critical issue is how quickly, and easily, you can recover. This involves applying mindfulness at two different points: (1) recognizing that you've become stressed; and (2) remembering to shift your attention from a state of being overwhelmed back to the task at hand. Mindfulness enhances both these steps. Recognizing the experience of stress draws on the same "noticing" skills that support mindful breathing. Consciously managing your stress involves "remembering" and "refocusing" as well. Modeling stress management in real-time supports your class directly and indirectly. This is true whether the stress is due to extraordinary circumstances or ordinary school-day challenges.

Stop Before You Start

One of the first potentially stressful elements of the school day occurs when teachers finish their own activities as students begin to arrive.

When you get to school, do you routinely turn on the computer, shuffle through papers to find something, or do any number of other routine, but necessary, tasks? If so, what usually happens when your students begin to arrive? Do you stop your activities immediately or do you glance at the clock and multitask in order to finish what you're doing and monitor the incoming class simultaneously?

My own natural temptation, and perhaps yours too, is to eke out every last minute before the school day officially begins in order to *get more things done.* The downside is that rushing to finish my multitasking often leaves me distracted, scrambling for my materials, and feeling generally annoyed. From there, its easy to feel angry about having to interrupt what you're doing—in much the same way students often feel irritable when told to put away something they're doing.

The alternative is to apply mindfulness and stop what you're doing even slightly before the schedule requires you to. Try setting an intention in the morning about this, and then support a positive outcome by picking tasks you can easily complete on time. Pace yourself realistically—especially if you only have a few minutes between getting to school and the students' arrival. You shouldn't need to get to school earlier than normal unless you absolutely have to accomplish something major before the official start of the school day.

Purposefully ensuring timely closure for your own pre-class activities is a potent investment in the quality of the incoming class. As a result you'll be present, in body and mind, when students arrive. Your ability to greet them with your full attention is a subtle yet powerful teaching strategy that often rapidly parlays into any of a number of desirable outcomes.

Students (like everyone else) are social beings who automatically check to see who is there and what is already happening as they enter the classroom. If they see you finishing various tasks, they're likely to pursue their own business and conversations until you call them to attention. In contrast, when you greet them as they walk in, you cue them to prepare for class through the quality of your attention. You set the tone and mark the transition from the period *before* class into the time *for* class. Then students walk through the door into a welcoming classroom climate that implicitly nudges them to shift their focus toward learning.

This approach assumes you are in the classroom before the students. However, the core principle applies even if you walk in after everyone else has arrived. Should you arrive after your students, do your best to wrap-up your tasks, conversations, and thoughts in the hallway before you enter the room. It's also well worth taking the extra thirty seconds or minute to pause and ground yourself before you walk through the door and switch your focus to your students.

Starting Class

Once you've shifted your attention to the students, you can assess the situation. This is what emergency responders do when they first arrive at the site of an emergency. It's also what talented public speakers do before saying a word to the audience. Assessing the situation begins with consciously gathering information and then using it to inform your subsequent actions. Mindfulness enhances this process since the first step to assessing the situation is, quite simply, noticing what's happening.

Taking at least one slow, deep, oxygenating breath prompts and paces the information-gathering phase. The information you gain during a few seconds or, at most, a minute will help you accurately perceive and effectively respond to your students. In particular, pay attention to whether they appear focused or distracted; energized or subdued; and ready for class or engaged in other activities. The quality of their presence provides you with clues to which methodology will work best this morning, as well as a reference point for measuring their progress as they transition from arriving to learning.

Once you've assessed the situation, you can select an appropriate strategy for actively engaging your students' attention. Simple traditions like saying "good morning" or taking attendance are often effective. Fun attention-grabbing approaches are also appropriate if your students are distracted but otherwise responsive. Creative strategies have a place in more challenging classes as well. However, it's important to keep in mind that students whose everyday behavior prevents them from participating in regular classrooms need specific curricular and behavioral support—even though they'll also benefit from your commitment to mindful teaching and teaching mindfulness.

Catching the attention of boisterous students in a regular classroom can be challenging, especially if doing so seems to require matching, if not exceeding, their energy level. Fortunately, there are more effective and less tiring alternatives. These strategies share a common capacity to attract and engage students' attention without imposing your authority over them and incurring the resistance and opposition that generally follow.

These techniques won't diminish your position as a teacher. Rather, they'll let you get to the other, more valuable, parts of class faster and more easily. Here are some strategies that alert students to the start of class and help them make the transition willingly.

- Signal you are ready to start class by flickering the lights.
- Begin class by ringing a chime or triangle, or playing a note on a xylophone or other reverberating instrument with a calming sound.
- Initiate a call-and-response sequence by clapping a specific rhythm and training your students to reply by repeating the rhythm with their own hands.
- Pose a riddle and engage students in solving the puzzle.
- Walk silently around the classroom, with a smile, and gently guide students into their seats using gestures or simple, safe touch.
- Take out something fascinating to look at and invite some students to begin examining it; then, as more and more students get interested, draw the others into the exploration process.
- Read a poem or lyrics from a song aloud every morning (you'll need to train your students to expect this); pick material that resonates with your class so they'll come to enjoy and appreciate the ritual of starting class with a reading.

Although these suggestions involve different methods, they all involve redirecting students' attention away from their own preoccupations and activities in attracting their interest with something else. As a result, students shift their focus because *they want to* and not (just) because you tell them to. They might not even notice they've made the transition into class. The sequence feels normal and natural—one minute they are socializing, the next they are trying to best their teacher by flawlessly imitating a clapping sequence or listening to a musical note. Learning and participating in class follows naturally.

None of these different modalities harness students' attention through a power struggle. On the other hand, when you simply demand that students stop talking to each other and listen, you implicitly foster a contest of wills. Although your need to begin class takes priority, the challenge is to do so without creating a dynamic in which students feel disempowered.

Communicating without using traditional "teacher" phrases is another advantage of these strategies. If you tell students to "Be quiet!" at the start of class, you might have a harder time engaging them later on. Verbally demanding silence requires you to speak over your students, countermanding previous— and future—efforts to enforce respectful communication. Since loudly calling "silence" is an oxymoron, actually *modeling* silence when students start talking to each other or shouting out answers during class works much more effectively. They'll notice if you stop speaking with them and become quiet on their own.

These strategies for transitioning to the start of class involve using energy and teaching techniques much the way some martial arts teach practitioners to use an opponent's own energy and momentum to gain control of the situation. In the classroom, it's much more productive to work consciously with your students' energy and redirect it, rather than set yourself up in opposition to it. When you are able to do this, you "shift their attention sideways," without opposing them head-on, and organically guide the class into "learning mode."

Take I for Students

Although the first transition of the school day has particular symbolic importance, other transitions (such as between classes) also provide opportunities to focus students' attention on the present moment. While some of the alternative approaches described earlier are interactive, few engage students in purposefully exercising their own mindfulness skills. If you want to teach mindfulness directly to your class, it's best to begin—as you did—with mindful breathing.

Appropriate at all grade levels, implementing "Take 1" for Mindful Breathing with students takes only a minute once they're familiar with the practice. However, at least initially, you'll need extra time to teach the basic progression and provide basic guidance on body position. Younger students appreciate very simple suggestions, whereas middle and high school students benefit from a modest amount of detail. It's best if you simply adapt the suggestions on posture found in Chapter 1 to meet your students' needs.

As you'll see, Take 1 is a slightly enhanced version of Take 5. In Take 1, though, you can use the sound of a musical note to initiate and conclude the students' version. You can use percussion instruments like the triangle or chime to make a simple reverberating sound or ring a note on a xylophone. The sound plays an important role in the classroom by indicating the parameters of the activity.

In Take 1, you (or eventually even a student) produce the sound of a single note, and everyone listens until it diminishes into silence. That transition marks the point at which students shift their attention from the external sound to the internal experience of mindful breathing. In addition to pacing the technique, the external sound provides an easy hook for attention that naturally draws their focus inward as the volume decreases. At the end of the progression, you produce the same sound to prompt your students to bring their awareness outward into the classroom.

TAKE I: MINDFUL BREATHING (FOR STUDENTS)

- Listen to the sound until it softens into silence.
- Switch your attention to noticing your breath.
- Breathe normally, paying attention to the feeling of the breath as it fills your lungs and then flows up and back out the way it came.
- Notice when you lose awareness of the breath and start thinking about something else, daydreaming, worrying, or snoozing.
- Bring your attention back to the breath.
- Return your awareness slowly to the classroom when you hear the sound marking the end of practice.

Considering Take I

You can decide how to introduce Take 1 to your students. One option is to engage them in a discussion to define mindfulness and catch their interest by explaining that mindful breathing can help them pay attention and make learning easier. Acknowledging that students are really busy, and their brains have to work very hard to keep track of everything, can help them see how training the mind to pay attention on purpose, from the inside, is relevant to them. Athletes, performing artists, and great thinkers benefit from using similar techniques—and your students can, too.

Another approach is to guide them experientially through the practice and then have a discussion on the value—or potential value—of the experience. You'll probably hear some students say mindful breathing felt relaxing or helped them calm down. You're just as likely to hear others comment that the technique was boring and almost put them to sleep. Others might comment that being silent and still felt really agitating. All these comments are normal, and you can encourage students to participate the next time, regardless of their initial experience.

Students are most likely to practice mindful breathing if you can find a seating arrangement that feels physically, mentally, and emotionally comfortable. Your class might want to sit cross-legged on the floor or remain seated at their desks facing forward. Sitting in a circle facing outward is another option. Sitting comfortably helps students focus on the breath, whereas discomfort is distracting.

Comfort is relevant to several other aspects of this activity, such as what students do with their eyes. It's important to give them the option of looking down or closing their eyes. Although either option would be acceptable to most students, some might feel uncomfortable with one or the other. This is particularly so for students who live with histories of trauma and abuse. Allowing them some control over how they find privacy will help them increase their comfort.

In addition, guiding them step-by-step through the practice will likely contribute to their sense of safety and ease by demonstrating you're right there with them. Your students will benefit from knowing you're in charge, especially if the activity involves new experiences. Your presence can reassure them that this activity is normal and safe, even if it seems unusual or discomfitting.

Students' minds are busy and their attention will wander— just like ours does. Reminding them (perhaps at intervals) to refocus on their breath helps them develop a mindfulness skill that supports academic learning. By practicing focusing and refocusing their attention, they internalize the process of noticing when they've become distracted and then remembering to re-engage. This will support them when they recognize they've read a page without knowing what's happened, or they've listened to instructions without hearing the content. Telling them it's okay if their attention wanders helps prevent them from getting distracted by unconstructive feelings about themselves when they realize they've lost focus. It's most important to emphasize that the activity is about practicing the same progression over and over again.

Simple though the sequence is, some students might have a hard time "getting" the experience of noticing the breath. Simply focusing on the breath may be too abstract. If so, suggest they notice how their chests rise and fall as the breath moves in and out of their lungs. Focusing on this physical sensation will help them learn to breathe deeply and provide the associated benefits. Also, even after the practice concludes, students are likely to continue breathing calmly and deeply, at least for a little while, which is healthy.

The quality of students' transition out of the progression is also important. Using a gentle sound supports a slow, balanced transition out of the technique back to full awareness of the classroom. Just as the sound led students into mindful breathing, it leads them out. Rushing them is counterproductive since they might feel disoriented and have a hard time concentrating afterward. In contrast, when students return to the present moment in their own time, their minds are undistracted. They are ready to learn.

You might find guiding students through this breathing technique also primes you to teach. Take 1 gives you a minute to take a little break, center yourself, and move intentionally forward. Your silent support and heightened presence will communicate to your students that this time is valuable and refreshing for you, too.

Riddles: Somewhere in Between

Just as you prompt students to place their attention at will, you can also create opportunities for them to learn about adjusting the intensity of their focus. Learning how to apply the proper level of concentration for any given task requires experience and time. Harnessing too much attention is often equally as counterproductive as investing inadequate effort. The most efficient level of focus requires a balance between the two extremes. In other words, you've got to make an effort—but to struggle is to try too hard.

This concept also pertains to mindfulness. The only way to develop the capacity to pay attention effectively is through practice. Firsthand experience of mindful breathing reveals what happens when concentration is too tight or too lax. If you apply too much focus, you'll experience mental distraction marked by hyper-awareness and constant thoughts (especially about how you're doing). Too little focus also leads to diminished results, and falls easily to distraction, forgetfulness, dullness, or sleepiness. These direct experiences emerge, over time, with mindfulness practice, but the learning curve is subtle.

In contrast, there are other practical, more immediate approaches that increase students' sensitivity to noticing—

and managing—different levels of effort. Physical activity is one of the best, from holding a pencil to playing sports. For example, draw students' attention to how they hold a pencil (or something similar). If they hold it too loosely, the pencil will wobble, and their writing will suffer. Grasping it too tightly leads to painful muscles and cramped writing. In contrast, maintaining steady but relaxed pressure is the most practical, sustainable, and effective way to hold a pencil.

Another useful analogy involves sports. Throwing a ball accurately requires focus, but too much focus interferes with the natural execution of the movement that propels the ball toward its target. Likewise, muscles need to be activated before a runner leaves the block, but too much tightness reduces speed. Even simple crafts offer powerful learning opportunities. Knitting too loosely leads to holes, but knitting too tightly results in an uncomfortable fit.

Mental activities increase sensitivity to identifying and applying the most effective level of focus, and riddles are among the best methodologies for teaching this type of mental balance. They are almost always captivating and tend to catalyze students' experience of "aha" moments of clear discovery. Although conventional knowledge and analysis contribute to the process, finding a riddle's solution requires students to find the balance between focusing their attention and expanding their awareness. This applies whether your students are kindergarteners or twelfth graders.

You can use existing developmentally appropriate riddles or develop your own. Working with a standard structure also provides a template that helps students create variations on their own. One approach involves selecting an object with multiple meanings and diverse uses. Then develop three statements about it using the basic structure, "If I were a (— — —), this object would (— — —)." Give these clues to students and ask them to find the identity of your object. Then consider their answers and eventually discuss the solution. Here is a fairly unremarkable and easily modeled example:

SAMPLE RIDDLE

- If I were a termite, this object would be my food.
- If I were a tired person, it would help me rest.
- If I were a child, it would give me a play structure.
- What am I?

Solution: a tree.

Straightforward and general as this riddle is, it nonetheless encourages students to explore different perspectives. This particular structure also reinforces another valuable lesson. They see that a single object can have multiple valid identities. A tree is no more or less "food" than it is a "play structure." Riddles also confront the reality that individuals offer diverse interpretations for the same object, usually based on different experiences and assumptions. Realizing that there can be more than one correct response to a question or situation builds tolerance of ambiguity and complexity, as well as supporting creativity.

Teaching methodologies work best when they accomplish multiple goals and strengthen different skills simultaneously. Riddles work well at the start of the day, or class, because they engage students' attention in a teacher-driven activity without overtly demanding that they conclude their own personal business. Riddles also promote creative thinking and receptivity—

valuable qualities that enhance learning in general. Some riddles, such as the previous example, allow you to teach "heavy" universal lessons in a "light" and clever way.

Working with riddles or any of the other strategies presented in this chapter, promotes students' readiness to learn by engaging their interest and inviting them to participate, consciously, in the present moment.

CHAPTER 4
How You See It

You must become aware of all things equally and not blinker yourself in order to concentrate on a particular subject.

Christopher Paolini, *Eldest*

SIGHT IS AS MUCH ABOUT EXTENDING ATTENTION OUTWARD as developing inner awareness, or insight. *How* you see relates to *what* you see, feel, and do, as well as how you communicate with others. Scientists, detectives, fashion designers, and architects all train their vision to facilitate their work. Artists do this, and so do athletes. So can your students and you.

One of the best opportunities for cultivating mindfulness of sight at school occurs just after you greet students, whether or not you've also implemented Take 1. While greetings are informal acknowledgments, taking attendance is a formal accounting of participation—but not necessarily a formality. Mindfully taking attendance can be meaningful. It includes making brief eye contact, and enables you to complete the transition into school mode while fulfilling one of your most basic responsibilities—figuring out *who has really showed up.*

Here!

Taking attendance can feel like drudgery, or it can provide a structure that prompts direct recognition between your students and you. This means you acknowledge each other—as you are in that moment—by making a visual and verbal connection. As a result, taking roll leads to two related positive outcomes: you'll know which students are physically present in your class, and also know who is "really there"—in body and in mind.

Enhancing the experience of roll call needn't require extra time. An instant of visual connection is often sufficient to form an invisible bridge with each student, one by one. When you complete roll call, you're connected with everyone and already in a position to draw the class's attention to you.

Imagine your ongoing communication with students during class moves like two-way traffic crossing tangible bridges. They focus on you, while you attend to them. Envisioning a model of these bridges facilitates dynamic interaction, whether you had set an intention to form those connections earlier in the day or you see them in your mind's eye as class begins.

Making eye contact with each student sends a significant symbolic message to the class. Looking up to see who is "here" reinforces that "being here" includes being involved, acknowledged, and valued. On the other hand, if you read the list of names and only look up when you don't hear an answer, you subtly signal "being absent" is somehow more noticeable than being present. Moreover, purposefully looking at each student, rather than solely responding to their verbal "here," "yeah," or "present," gives you additional subtle information about them.

Verbal greetings enhance the visual. Names can serve as proxies for flesh-and-blood students during roll call or they can convey respect and recognition by acknowledging another facet of a person's identity. Over-analyzing roll call is impractical, but touching on this particular issue emphasizes an important point. Intention determines whether a gesture or statement enhances or weakens human connections. The way you say a student's name can confer welcome and attention or dismissal—literally and figuratively.

I pay extra attention to greeting my students for two reasons. The first, as mentioned above, concerns their experience: I want them to feel that being "here" is important—not just physically, but also mentally and emotionally. On a fundamental level, I believe their physical presence isn't enough.

My second reason is more self-serving, but still beneficial for them. I can't teach academic content effectively to a class of sleepy, distracted, or emotionally overwhelmed students. If I try, we'll all end up frustrated and unhappy. I need to know what's happening with my students before I begin teaching the lesson.

Applying mindfulness to taking roll gives me a dedicated time during which to assess my class's presence, and that, in turn, increases my efficacy as a teacher. If I notice my students are physically there, but energetically absent, I can respond appropriately and help bring them back. Doing so provides more promising conditions for teaching and learning.

Noticing the quality of students' presence and responding accordingly communicates how much you value their conscious involvement—not just with your words—but with your attention and your actions. This models one of the most basic lessons in life. You will teach, and your students will learn, that "showing up" is about really seeing and really being seen.

Attending to What's Important

Mindfulness while taking roll emphasizes the value of full presence, and the role of attention is its root. Attention is a system that lets your brain prioritize and process information according to relevance. Basically, attention enables you to focus on what's useful without being distracted by information that isn't.

If you're good at paying attention, you can probably focus on whatever you want, whenever you want. If paying attention feels challenging, you're likely to exert extra effort to concentrate, and you might still find yourself easily and frequently distracted. This happens because lower priority information takes center-stage. It "grabs" your attention and you lose focus on whatever you had previously prioritized.

Attention is critical for success at school; fortunately, both teachers and students can cultivate stronger attention. With practice, you can improve your ability to stay focused, notice when you've lost focus, and refocus at will. Mindful seeing techniques, such as the observation technique presented later in this chapter, directly contribute to training attention and improving short-term memory.

Mindfulness also reduces mind-wandering. Less mind-wandering means you are able to return to a stream of thought more easily after an interruption. So, when a student calls out mid-way through a detailed explanation, you can respond appropriately and pick up where you left off. Strengthening the skills that reduce mind-wandering also helps your students notice when they're daydreaming so they can refocus and stay on task.

Mindfulness has another benefit—it strengthens the process of prioritizing between relevant and irrelevant information. This happens when you watch for thoughts and emotions, and acknowledge their presence without engaging in their content. It also happens when students concentrate on learning despite activity in the background. So, even though students can physically *see* other people and things in the classroom, mindful seeing helps them look at the blackboard and ignore other visual distractions.

Mindful Memory

There are numerous possible classroom-based mindful seeing techniques from which to choose, and even more avenues to extend class discussion beyond methodology. The following paragraphs highlight two different approaches. First, you'll examine how to infuse a traditional observation technique with mindfulness. Then you'll learn how to implement a discrete technique that promotes mindful seeing among students. Both activities work well with students at all grade levels, although of course it's important to adjust the challenge and sophistication of the follow-up discussion to meet your students' needs.

Memory games pervade the mainstream, but infusing them with mindfulness can increase their efficacy. Traditionally, it's been more important to demonstrate how much the students remember rather than focus their attention on the experience of memorizing. In other words, these activities emphasize outcomes over process. Even so, over time and with repetition, memorization skills tend to improve. The stated goals are reached, but the means remain subservient to the ends.

Cultivating mindfulness offers another approach to memory games that yields the same, if not better, outcomes, while emphasizing the *process of memorization* as the key to success.

Such a practice prioritizes the experience of paying attention and allows students to investigate factors within themselves that promote or interfere with focusing. One of the most powerful ways to teach differences between these approaches is to provide the opportunity for comparison and experiential learning. Begin by implementing Mindful Memory, a simple traditional game that emphasizes the outcomes. The sequence of steps is fairly simple.

First, when your students aren't looking, assemble a dozen distinct objects and put them on an otherwise empty table. Cover them with a cloth, and invite students to gather around the table so that everyone has a clear view.

Then remove the cloth and allow the class to look at the objects for a minute without doing anything else. After the allotted time, cover the objects again, and ask the students to recall as many objects as possible from memory and list them on a piece of paper without speaking to each other. Once everyone is done, invite the students to compare their lists with reality (uncover the objects) and discuss the experience. The accuracy of the students' responses will indicate whether you need to simplify the activity or increase the degree of difficulty the next time around.

The second phase begins once you've completed the traditional approach. Begin immediately or on the next day. In this phase, you'll employ a series of variations to prompt students to cultivate mindfulness about the process of observing and use their results as another form of information that contributes to analyzing personal experience.

The first variation of Mindful Memory requires placing a new group of objects under the cloth and includes a warm-up phase of mindful breathing before removing the cloth. You can implement Take 1 or a similar progression to guide students to calm their minds and focus their attention prior to observing the objects. After concluding the mindful breathing phase, repeat the steps of the game as previously described. Then consider the results on the students' lists as well as their inner experience. Did Take 1 affect the outcome and/or the quality of the process? If so, it can be fruitful ask students to discuss their theories as to why this may be so.

The second variation provides another perspective that deepens understanding and discussion. This time, set up the objects on a side table before class and begin teaching class normally. When the class is fully engaged in the topic, stop unexpectedly, gather students around the side table, and uncover the objects. Move students immediately into the observation phase and complete the basic steps. During your discussion, ask students to describe the experience of rapidly switching their focus without prior notice. How accurate were their results?

So far students have experienced the effects of calming the mind prior to close observation and the results of interrupting and redirecting focused attention without notice. The last variation provides them with the opportunity to examine the effects of distraction and multitasking on concentration. This time play some music or read a compelling story aloud while students observe a new set of objects. This approach forces them to focus on completing their task despite their awareness of competing stimuli. Again, discuss what happened experientially and consider the accuracy of students' lists.

Once you've completed all the variations, ask the class to discuss—or perhaps write about—what they learned through their individual experiences and actual comparison. Ask them to describe the connections between close observation and memory, as well as a calm mind and attention. Then go one step further, and challenge students to apply their conclusions to real-life situations.

The idea is to guide them to extend specific lessons to other contexts. Ask them to describe their optimal conditions for taking an important test—given what they've learned about promoting or weakening attention. What about doing homework or performing athletics? Or when they listen to someone telling them something important—are they more likely to remember what they've been told when they calm their minds first? What happens when they interrupt doing something really compelling because they've been ordered to listen, or when they try to listen while focusing on another task?

Mindful Memory strengthens conventional outcomes (students list the objects with increased accuracy) and, even more importantly, triggers powerful learning about sight, mental state, and attention. The approach works with children of all ages, instilling an understanding of attention as a dynamic skill. Reinforcing this principle deepens the benefit of the learning and can also add to the fun of discovery.

Field of Vision

Where you look directly affects what you see. I can, for instance, easily overlook something important that's right in front of me when I assume that it has to be somewhere else. And of course this myopia is about mental shortsightedness and has nothing to do with my functional vision. At home, my children laugh when I shuffle through the papers on my desk like a tornado, looking for a picture that's visible on the shelf nearby—where I'm quite sure "it can't be." Their amusement lessens my discomfort, but the close ties between assumption and perception are not so funny when the stakes are high and I can't see what I'm looking for.

What you *expect* to see also affects what you *notice* by defining your field of vision. It's easy to wear mental blinkers based on past experience and assumptions without even realizing they are there. Sometimes the disconnect between actual reality and a pre-constructed mental image leads to more significant oversights and lessening of possibilities. This section will present an exercise that addresses this phenomenon.

The Field of Vision activity provides students of all ages with a safe and fun opportunity to explore "blinker-vision" and learn from their experience. The set up is very simple, although you'll need to take your class outdoors to an unobstructed piece of ground covered with many little twigs. Delineate an area for the activity and ask the students to come within that space so they gather around you. Select and display a three-inch twig from the ground and explain that you are about to place that twig somewhere in the designated space. The point of the activity is for students to locate that twig, in silence, and without helping each other. Ask them to let you know, *silently,* by meeting your eyes, when they've identified the twig and then step outside the area as other students continue the search.

Once you present these directions, ask students to step outside the activity space, face away from you, and close their eyes so you can place the twig without observation. Walk around the area bending down frequently as if you were putting the twig on the ground. In reality, place the twig behind your ear (like a pencil) and be sure that an inch protrudes, visibly, toward your face. You don't need to make it obvious, but it should be noticeable if someone were to look at your face directly. Then ask students to begin looking while you remain within the designated space, walking slowly and looking down.

Your students will swarm into the space, noses to the ground, searching for the twig. Some will feel frustrated very quickly, whereas others will become totally absorbed in the activity. When students pick up different twigs and show them to you, meet their gaze and shake your head "no." Someone, perhaps even very quickly, will notice the twig behind your ear and indicate that they've solved the puzzle. Simply nod to that student and continue walking in the area while he or she moves to stand on the outside perimeter. When this happens, some students will look at you and see the twig, while others will feel even more pressured to look closely at the ground. Allow students to search until everyone "gets it" (or until you perceive students begin to feel uncomfortable—either because they're tired of waiting or they're self-conscious about not having found the twig).

At that point, conclude the activity by taking the twig out from behind your ear and asking students to gather around you, again, for a brief discussion. Ask them, "What was the point of this activity?" and "What did you learn?" Their answers, regardless of age, are likely to reflect some degree of self-awareness regarding the connections between assumptions and vision. They will acknowledge looking on the ground because "that's where twigs are" rather than behind your ear because "who expects anyone to put a twig behind their ear?"

They are likely to explain that the point of the activity is to show how thinking affects seeing. Extend the discussion by exploring the relationship between missing the "correct answer" because of having preconceptions about the "nature of that answer." Invite your students to offer their own examples of this principle, and then challenge them to identify and use protective strategies that reduce the occasions of wearing blinkers unknowingly.

Mindful Seeing

Applying mindfulness to sight is an antidote for wearing the blinkers of assumptions. As with the memory game, the following Mindful Seeing activity asks for increased observation, attention, and memory. It also incorporates lessons from Field of Vision regarding the importance of looking directly, without the lens of expectation or assumption. Unlike these other two activities, Mindful Seeing simply emphasizes the experience of mindfulness in the context of seeing, and it works best if students are already familiar with mindful breathing.

Mindful Seeing includes a basic progression along with several variations. The basic methodology provides a structured task that prompts students of all ages to experience the process of *looking* at something and noticing what happens after the first instant of visual perception. The direct experience of seeing—and the simultaneous awareness of the experience of seeing—is mindfulness. Noticing what happens immediately afterward, when you start thinking about what you see—applying names, making comparisons, or developing ideas—is about applying mindfulness.

The difference between mindful seeing and applying mindfulness to seeing is analogous to mindful breathing and the experience of applying mindfulness when thoughts emerge while watching the breath. Mindfulness is the unified experience of paying attention to awareness. Applying mindfulness is about training, and it happens once you experience awareness of "self" and the specific "object" of attention.

Mindful seeing is what happens in the first moment of looking at something where the viewer (you), the action (looking), and the object (whatever you're looking at) merge into a comprehensive experience without words or concepts. This happens, sometimes for only a nearly imperceptible instant, before you attach labels like "an apple" or adjectives such as "green" or "bruised" or thoughts about it, like "I'd like to eat that." You simply see, and your awareness pervades the seeing and your attention focuses on whatever is there. Mindfulness can move through the experience from mindful seeing to mindfully noticing as your attention shifts and you become aware of processing what you see.

Since mindfulness develops through personal experience and practice, implementing an activity and following it up with discussion and explanation tends to engage students most effectively. Here is a basic progression that introduces mindful seeing to students by guiding them to focus on something edible (like an apple) or an attractive object (such as an interesting pebble). You'll need a sufficient number of the same type of object (a bag of apples or pebbles, for example) to distribute among the class. If possible, use objects that you're comfortable giving to the students after the activity. Begin the activity by distributing one object per student from your bag and then guide students through the progression below:

MINDFUL SEEING (FOR STUDENTS)

- Hold the object in your hands.
- Get to know your object just by looking at it. (Give students about one minute.)
- Look more closely and examine its characteristics,

such as shape, color, texture, and marks. (Give students about two minutes.)
- Return your attention to looking at your object, if you become distracted.
- Place your object in the bag. (Collect the objects and then place all of them on a table.)
- Come up to the table, and examine all the objects without touching them until you recognize the one you looked at earlier.
- Pick up the object and take it back to your seat.

Once you've concluded the progression, it's important to specify whether you plan to collect the objects or allow the students to keep them. For the sake of food safety and hygiene, it's best to use fruit once and then let the students have—and even eat—their own piece. However, you can easily recycle pebbles or similar objects, or give them to your students as gifts.

After you finish the lesson progression, and everyone is settled in their seats again, initiate a class discussion. In particular, focus on whether students experienced any difference between "getting to know the object by looking at it" and "examining the object's characteristics." The main issue here is to draw attention to distinguishing between *looking at* something and *looking for* something. Simply observing the object is looking for the sake of looking, whereas noticing specific details has a purpose.

Once they grasp this point, you can encourage explorations of its implications. Ask your students, "What happens when you just look at a person versus when you see if a person has certain physical characteristics?" Or, "Is there a difference between seeing something and forming an opinion about it?"

Considering these questions can be challenging, as much because distinguishing between *looking at* and *looking for* something is unfamilar as because realizing the degree to which our thoughts and attitudes influence *what* and *how* we see.

As students reflect on the experience of looking, guide them to consider the role of close, patient observation. Begin by acknowledging that, at first glance, all the objects probably looked very similar. At one level, that is indeed true. However, you can point out that through close observation it was possible, if not probable, that students would find distinguishing characteristics.

This point can facilitate a deeper discussion about first impressions. Begin by asking students, "What happens when you look at a book, realize you don't like the cover or the first page and put it down for good?" They're likely to answer that you might miss a good read! Then build from there inquiring, "What happens when you look at people and make assumptions about them based on what you see?" Your students are all quite likely to know what this experience feels like. Almost everyone knows, because it happens all the time.

Consider your own experiences with first impressions. Have you walked into a class on the first day of school, seen all those bright shiny smiling faces and decided that you've got "easy" students only to realize a few days later that they aren't so easy? What about when a new student looks like a previous student whose disruptive behavior was exhausting? Do you look at the new student with fresh eyes, or do you automatically remember the other student and recall negative feelings and assumptions that have no current basis? How often do you—or does anyone—*see what's really here*, right now, or is *what we think is here* based on a subtle process of superimposing meanings from the past onto the present?

Consider relating a personal—or even hypothetical—experience to your class to provide a powerful approach to illustrating the potential outcomes associated with mistaking a first impression for reality. It's important to pick an appropriate example that implicitly sets a safe tone and respectful boundaries to contain the class discussion. Once you've launched the discussion, inquire whether your students have had the experience of meeting someone for the first time and immediately (or belatedly) realizing that they instinctively formed an opinion about this stranger based on his or her superficial likeness to a familiar person.

Almost everyone knows how this feels because it's so easy to make rapid assumptions based on past experience. Powerful memories can strongly influence present attitudes and actions and affect your ability to look at someone new with openness. Students of all ages, K–12, can explore the relationships between *how they look at people* and *what they actually see*.

Some middle school students, and most high school students, can grasp the difference between mindful seeing and looking through the lens of past experience. Just as developing skill with mindful breathing requires practice, mindful seeing also relies on familiarity derived from repetition. As you—and they—become more facile with *just looking*, you'll become more sensitive to noticing the point at which pure *looking* ends and *thinking and deciding* or *attributing meaning* begins.

Pause

What you see can profoundly affect how you feel—even before you have the time to think. I feel better when I teach in a clean, bright, and spacious classroom, and worse when my class is held in a dreary, windowless space. I experience a wave of anger and sadness when I first see how students have defaced school property. When I observe older students patiently assisting younger children, I'm quick to feel pride and pleasure.

Experiencing rapid emotions is fine. Potential difficulties arise when these experience trigger an equally fast behavioral and/or emotional chain-reaction that might, with hindsight, prove unconstructive. The almost instantaneous feeling of fear that appears when you notice a car zooming toward you can prompt you to move quickly and possibly save your life. The wave of anger that bears down on you when you see something that looks like a brawl might instigate a prompt reaction which makes sense at the time, but turns out to be inappropriate when the drama teacher intervenes and explains that the tousling students were rehearsing—and under supervision.

The root issue here is the fact that the brain naturally responds to sensations, including visual input, with emotions first and rational thoughts later. It's a kind of default setting that kicks in automatically unless you purposefully train your mind to function differently.

An alternative setting involves practicing mindfulness (so you notice what's happening, as it's happening) and consciously taking a very brief pause between registering *what's happening* and *doing something with or about it*. Purposefully taking a breath both initiates and paces this pause. So, as soon as you see the group of students "fighting" and begin to feel intense emotions, extend your mindfulness and take a breath. The time it takes to complete one cycle of inhalation and exhalation gives your thinking mind the chance to catch up with your feelings, and enables you to choose advisedly in what manner you want to respond.

The pause, even if only transient, can make all the difference by giving you time to determine: (1) the simple facts you perceive without the overlay of emotion or interpretation; (2) how you feel about what you see; (3) what you think about it; and (4) what might be best to do. This is a four-step sequence that involves sight, emotions, thoughts, and finally action. When you skip the third step—thoughts—you risk a knee-jerk response that may or may not serve you well. Pausing is the key, because doing so buys time for thoughts to catch up and collaborate with emotions to form a constructive plan.

With practice, mindfulness pervades this four-step sequence and even helps afterward. At first you are aware of what you see and feel. Then you remember to pause, and watch as thoughts arise. Finally, you synthesize the information at hand—both the feelings and the thoughts—to make, and implement, a plan for your next step. Once the sequence concludes, it's time to move on, physically, mentally, and emotionally. Applying mindfulness to reducing emotional arousal promotes a faster and easier recovery. The more effective your self-calming process, the greater your ability to "bounce back" after an intense experience.

Practicing mindfulness *when you're not swept away by emotion* is the precursor to applying mindfulness in the midst of real-life situations. For example, the *experience of seeing* something neutral, like an apple or a pebble, is comparatively free of distractions compared with looking at a person toward whom you have strong, negative feelings. This is why practicing with neutral objects is the first phase. Then, once your students—and you—become more familiar with the experience of "just seeing," you can increase the challenge by looking at something or someone that holds a charge of positive or negative personal meaning.

As you work with applying mindfulness to observing more emotionally "loaded" objects, your skill in using this technique, spontaneously in real-time, will improve. Eventually, the experience of mindful seeing cues your attention to focus on the four-step sequence that begins with seeing.

Training the mind to pay attention to breathing, or seeing, improves your ability to pay attention to the experience of feeling. Breathing and seeing happen so naturally that it's easy to take them for granted. Emotions are much the same—they come and go, often taking you by surprise. However, the greater your ability to notice your emotions as soon as possible, the more likely you are to pause, think, and act with mindfulness.

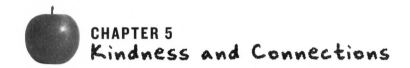

CHAPTER 5
Kindness and Connections

[U]nderstanding begets empathy and compassion,
even for the meanest beggar in the meanest city of
Alagaësia.

Christopher Paolini, *Eldest*

EARLY IN MY CAREER, a mentor told me that success in any field
is "all about relationships." At the time, quite frankly, I
thought he was daft. I have since come to see how very wrong
I was. In fact this simple statement acknowledges reality in
the classroom. Academic performance improves when students feel safe and connected—in short, when they are supported by a strong relationship with their teacher.

Most teachers want students to like and respect them and
students want the same from their teachers. It's easier to teach
when a class is receptive, just as it's easier to learn when the
teacher is supportive. So the challenge is to connect mindfully
with students in ways that support optimal learning—by
building relationships characterized by respect and open communication. Once the terms of the connection between the
teacher and students are clear and contextualized, mutual

appreciation and caring can follow, and that in turn further nurtures the connection.

Mindfulness promotes inner awareness and outer attunement in tandem. The more easily, and accurately, you notice what's happening mentally, emotionally, and physically within you, the less effort you need to expend paying attention to yourself. As a result, your inner awareness parlays into more energy for focusing on other people's experiences. This occurs when people communicate with reciprocal awareness and attention, and in the classroom this means teachers and students interact in sync.

Student Buy-In

Even if you are convinced that mindfulness has a place in school, your students may not have the same confidence. "Mindfulness" might sound strange, foreign, or hokey. Although mindfulness techniques can add novelty, they can also elicit resistance due to unfamiliarity. Your class's developmental stage and the nature of your relationship with your students will strongly influence their willingness to try something "different."

Typically, younger students (K–5) like participating in classroom-based mindfulness activities out of curiosity or simply because the teacher presents them—and following is what younger students do. If an introductory mindfulness technique is pleasant or interesting, they will gladly do it again. Even if it wasn't, they are still likely to give it a second chance, especially if you alter the technique to increase novelty. Elementary school students generally savor diversity of experience and welcome activities that postpone "regular" schoolwork.

In contrast, middle and high school students can often be wary of unfamiliar techniques, especially if participation threatens their sense of propriety. After all, practicing mindful breathing, listening, and seeing are not typical classroom activities. Pre-teens and teens are acutely sensitive to doing things that might be somehow "weird."

Despite the possibility of initial resistance, mindfulness practice can contribute significantly to the learning environment in middle and high school classrooms. Once older students "buy in" and participate they have the potential to benefit more than less mature students. The main challenge with older students is presenting mindfulness practice as something "desirable" so as to motivate them to overcome their hesitation or reluctance and try something "different."

Your own buy-in plays a critical role in normalizing mindfulness practice at the middle and high school level. While keeping the details of your personal experience with mindfulness or other forms of meditation private is advisable, you will communicate your attitude toward mindfulness practice implicitly through the quality of your teaching presence and the manner of your explanations. And your sudents will notice.

Students in the fifth to twelfth grades typically care whether mindfulness can be useful *to them*. In other words they want to know, "How will mindfulness help me get what *I* want?" Some students will find resonance with the links between mindfulness and skills that facilitate success in disciplines such as academics, athletics, or the arts. Others will be more interested in the connection between mindfulness practice and satisfying relationships, personal health, and stress reduction.

There's one basic catch to cultivating students' "buy in" for mindfulness practice: you can only take the intellectual discussion so far without first-hand experience and students are often reluctant to try something "different" before they understand its purpose. Nonetheless, acknowledging this paradox can help move things forward. You might need to have an introductory discussion, and then invite students to try mindful breathing, and then return to brainstorming with them about practical applications.

Students will have a reference point for exploring this issue after they've tried Take 1 or Mindful Seeing, and you can prompt them to stretch their minds as needed. Ask them if they agree that "Mindful breathing can help people calm down," and inquire whether a calm mind affects the ease, and quality, of their schoolwork.

Another strategy is to suggest that students experiment to see whether engaging in a brief mindfulness practice before a test leads to stress reduction and better results. The combination of guided discussions and classroom experiments works well to promote those "aha" moments when students experientially and intellectually connect mindfulness with reaching their own goals.

Cultivating student buy-in requires both finesse and special sensitivity toward empowering them to take ownership of their interest and practice. Your primary role is to introduce the topic and jump-start their learning process by involving them in some exploratory activities. As you engage older students in discussion, consciously phrase your examples to relate directly to them—and downplay your own experiences. De-personalizing the topic gives your students the freedom to have their own experiences with mindfulness without concern that you might compare their practice with your own. Their practice is about them, and your words can powerfully reinforce their confidence with boundaries.

Students understand you have the responsibility to provide many different learning opportunities conducive to the process of their intellectual discovery and social and emotional learning. As a result, they'll have some level of openness to viewing mindfulness as another one of these topics. You can reinforce this openness by demonstrating that you are offering mindfulness practice to them without any personal agenda. If they like it, that's fine, and you can expand your applications in the classroom. If they don't like working with mindfulness techniques, that's fine too. You can still infuse your own teaching experience with mindfulness, and doing so will meaningfully support your students without requiring them to participate overtly in the practice.

If your students don't relate to actual mindfulness techniques or show interest in intellectual discussions about the related outcomes, it's time to try a different approach. One option is to engage middle and high school students in exploring their own work habits, and through doing so shift their attention away from the techniques (which they might label "boring" or "useless") to the real life benefits of applying the skills *that develop with mindfulness practice.* Invite them to consider their own experience and respond to questions such as:

- Do you concentrate best while alone, in a quiet room, or in the midst of activity?
- Are you most productive while sitting at a desk, on the sofa, or on the floor?
- Is homework easiest right after school, or do you need a break?
- Do you work better in sprints (maybe ten minutes followed by some kind of a break) or marathons (working for up to an hour before taking a break)?

All of these questions prompt self-reflection and involve noticing direct experience. In fact, answering the questions involves mindfulness, but using that term isn't necessary. As you explore the answers to these questions, you are likely to find that responses vary dramatically. Some students work best individually and in total quiet, whereas others need background noise and activity to support their focus. You're likely to have students who memorize by writing and rewriting the text, and others who need to pace and exclaim as loudly as possible. Although specific personal answers are significant to students individually, the experience of looking for the answers is even more important. Whether or not students embrace the term "mindfulness" is ultimately unimportant when compared with the learning that comes through increasing self-awareness and self-reflection.

Strategies for Settling

Attending to students' learning styles is as valuable and practical for them as it is for you as their teacher. The probability of academic success increases if students know what works best for them and are able to communicate their needs to you. Furthermore, the more insight you gain, the more likely it is you will be able to validate their needs and guide students to find appropriate and effective learning strategies. Students often lack confidence that teachers empathize with their challenges—especially when those challenges seem to impact the teacher negatively.

Consider what happens when you're ready to start class and your students are perpetually tardy when returning from another activity. It's likely they feel distracted and unsettled and your acknowledgment that their previous teacher always dismisses them late doesn't get them into your room any sooner. It's also likely the tension level is high although no one openly examines what's really going on. Your challenge is to make the most of the time that you do have, without increasing their anxiety or feeding your own frustration.

You can view the reality of their late arrival as a major inconvenience for everyone, or as a teachable moment. If you give them a pop quiz as soon as they arrive, you're likely to catch them at a disadvantage and their performance will probably suffer. Instead, you can recognize the tension directly and address the situation openly, saying something like, "I want to start class successfully, so I will speak with (the other teacher) about releasing you earlier, but let's talk about what would help you focus once you get here."

With your prompting, they're likely to recognize they need strategies to help them shift mentally and emotionally as they move physically from the previous class into yours. Perhaps the time between classes is simply too short for a leisurely pace, and, in all likelihood, they're going to feel "wound up" by the time they arrive. Even if you can't change the constraints of that reality, you can still work with it more productively. Ask them if they want to take thirty seconds to catch their breath silently when they reach your room. Or suggest that you'll give your quizzes at the end of class, demonstrating that mindfulness about current experience can guide behavior—yours and theirs.

Some classes simply need to burn off some energy in order to sit still. If your students tell you their thinking improves after physical activity, you might experiment with running them through a few minutes of exercises and stretches before you expect them to settle down. The health and attention benefits derived from movement usually more than make up for time lost from traditional learning. In addition, giving them a few minutes to move communicates respect and caring through implicitly validating and responding directly to their needs.

While intense movement works beautifully for some students, others thrive when the classroom feels like a quiet and safe haven. If your students are over-stimulated when they arrive, they'll need to calm down enough to concentrate effectively before they can learn. Once they, and you, realize this, you can help them regain their grounding by playing gentle music, establishing a rule that they enter the classroom in silence, or inviting them to observe a new object in the room, such as a shell, flowers, or even a picture of the universe.

In the elementary grades, a nature table provides a wonderful object for attention. There's no need to change the objects daily, but it's best to introduce new rocks, leaves, or other common natural objects frequently enough that students' interest won't wane. At the beginning of class, invite students to go to the nature table and select an object to observe briefly. Then, once they sit at their desks, ask them to see the object they just studied in their minds' eyes.

Occasionally, you might encourage them to identify an attractive aspect of their object and imagine cultivating that quality within themselves. For example, a soft branch in the springtime bends during storms without breaking and some students might want to become more flexible. Others might like the way light passes through a sliver of rock showing unexpectedly beautiful patterns and they might want to nurture hidden treasures in their personality. They can keep these observations private or share them with the class. Although the whole activity takes less than five minutes, the resulting mental calm can pervade the remainder of the lesson period.

Or, if your class wants to be "drawn in" to the academic content, you have the chance to meet their needs and simultaneously cultivate other skills. Try beginning each class with a very brief daily reading. You might create a roster that rotates the responsibility for picking a quote from an anthology of sayings or poems, and presenting the selection orally to the class. Everyone participates in the rotation both by paying attention to the presenter and occasionally presenting. The regular readings help students become present and nurture their confidence speaking to an audience.

These are just a few ways to activate students' mindfulness about how best to cue their attention at the start of class. Using methodologies that validate their own insights as they develop their concentration skills builds students' confidence in the value of self-awareness. Students crave opportunities to participate in structuring their classroom experience. Mindfulness fosters and maximizes these occasions.

Intangible Qualities

Buy-in for mindfulness practice grows from awareness of the experiences and things people value. The most tangible ones are the easiest to name: academic success, athletic performance, and artistic achievement. Intangible qualities are often valued even more, but they are so basic as to be overlooked. People want happiness. We don't want to live in pain. We all crave kindness, empathy, and compassion. These qualities enhance the tangible measures of success, and in their absence even the greatest achievements can feel empty and unimportant.

Kindness is a feeling of emotional generosity. It can extend toward the self with a wish that we ourselves experience happiness and well-being. We can also extend that wish beyond the self toward others. Kindness tends to bring pleasure and warm-heartedness both to the person generating and extending the quality and to those who receive it.

Kindness begins with intention and can take a multitude of forms. Sometimes kindness seems harsh, as in the "tough love" approach to working with youth-at-risk. Or kindness can appear warm and fuzzy, exemplified by the caring attention that comforts a distressed child.

Empathy supports kindness by enabling you to know how someone else feels. Empathy is the capacity to extend your awareness beyond your personal reality and experience the world through someone else's mind, heart, and body. It relies on the assumption of interconnectedness; people have common experiences. With empathy, your pain is my pain, and your joy becomes my joy.

Knowing how your students feel helps you work with them more effectively, especially in challenging situations. "Trying on" their feelings, without losing sight of your own identity, improves social and emotional skillfulness in the classroom. Not only do you develop greater insight into their needs, you can use that insight to inform your offers of assistance.

Compassion and kindness are two sides of the same coin. Both aim to promote happiness. Compassion does so indirectly by decreasing pain, whereas kindness promotes happiness directly. The capacity to extend kindness and/or compassion toward others effectively has a lot to do with attunement—that state of being in sync with another person.

Cultivating Kindness

Many people experience kindness as a byproduct of mindfulness practice. Purposefully generating and extending kindness naturally enhances this outcome. The more you feed the flame of kindness, the greater your warmth and capacity to radiate it to others.

The first step is to take a few minutes to practice mindful breathing. Purposefully fostering concentration and heightened awareness leads to an inner state conducive to generating and experiencing kindness. Then take a minute or more to repeat the Kindness Reflections below (or your adaptation of them) silently or aloud. When you're ready to stop repeating them, you can simply remain alert, but restful, without any particular object of attention, or you can return your awareness to mindful breathing.

KINDNESS REFLECTIONS (FOR TEACHERS)

- May I feel joy.
- May I heal from pain.
- May I find peace.
- May I gain greater wisdom and skill.

This progression of four reflections begins with the wish for joy, which is an expression of kindness toward the self. The desire to heal from pain is about directing compassion inward toward oneself. The hope for peace supports kindness as well as compassion. Finally, the intention to gain greater wisdom and skill focuses on developing both a strategy and the capacity for cultivating the first three reflections.

Although the Kindness Reflections send kindness toward the self, they also extend beyond and through the self toward others. My happiness can bring joy to others. My healing from pain can also reduce other people's suffering on my behalf and thus reduce the pain I inadvertently cause others.

If I live in peace, those around me will benefit as well—and I can bring my greater wisdom and skill into my actions and relationships.

Once you've practiced the kindness technique of focusing on yourself, you might wish to change the wording and intention to offer the same wishes to those you love. So, the next version of the technique could sound something like this:

KINDNESS REFLECTIONS FOR LOVED ONES (FOR TEACHERS)

- May my loved ones feel joy.
- May my loved ones heal from pain.
- May my loved ones find peace.
- May my loved ones gain greater wisdom and skill.

After practicing with the Kindness Reflections for Loved Ones, you can choose to extend goodwill toward others such as people for whom you have neutral and even negative feelings. Imagine that you are at the center of a circle surrounded by rings of people; those closest are dearest, and those on the farthest ring are people toward whom you have antipathy.

It's important to begin using this kindness technique while focusing on yourself. As you cultivate your capacity for generating—and receiving—joy, healing from pain, and so on, you will also increase your ability to generate and direct the same wishes toward others. Start with your loved ones, and then, moving at your own pace, extend these wishes to the other people in the rings further and further away from the center.

The next series of reflections could focus on a neutral person, "May my neighbors feel joy," and eventually lead to many neutral people, "May everyone in my country feel joy." Another progression moves from "May my loved ones feel joy" to "May my colleagues and students feel joy" on to "May _____ (someone you find frustrating or difficult) feel joy," and eventually, should you feel ready, to "May _____ (someone you absolutely despise or of whom you feel resentful or jealous) feel joy."

You might experience some discomfort wishing the best for people toward whom you have neutral or negative feelings. It can be very challenging even to consider extending compassion, much less kindness, toward someone who has deeply hurt you or your loved ones. Don't worry if you don't think you can go that far. Just take it one circle at a time, and keep attending to your experience in the moment as you practice this technique. At the same time, also try not to get caught up in any storylines that arise in you.

I encourage you to approach kindness practice with curiosity and openness. Commit to trying it for at least a few days, or a couple of weeks, before deciding whether it offers any value for you. With regular practice, you might notice an increasing sense of inner happiness or contentment. You might also begin to find alternative ways of handling people and situations you've had difficulty with in the past.

Kindness practice amplifies the capacity to help other people manage their own pain and challenges. Increased confidence smoothes the steps from kindness to empathy and then compassion. The benefits also extend in the other direction so that sharing, if not rejoicing, in others' happiness and accomplishments becomes even more natural and fulfilling.

Noticing Kindness

Mindfully engaging in kindness practice does not automatically paint the world with pretty "kindness" colors that distort reality. Instead, you're likely to find that your *sensitivity* to the presence of kindness—in and around you—intensifies. Not only does this mean you recognize specific acts of kindness more easily, but also you are more likely to notice unexpected *opportunities* to act kindly. There isn't more *ambient* kindness; it's just that you become more attuned to it among colleagues, family members, friends, and even strangers.

Like you, students can also train their capacity for experiencing and extending kindness. Whereas adults tend to begin with a mental kindness practice, like the one presented earlier, students often find action a more effective context for cultivating kindness. One approach is to assign a defined task such as to perform several acts of kindness and identify a few acts of kindness demonstrated by other people. This task prompts students to learn by *doing*.

Noticing kindness—inside and around them—helps students in all grades link mindfulness with personal, community, and even global connections. Your students probably have a sense of global environmental, political, and economic issues. They may have heard some version of the statement that when a butterfly beats its wings in Asia, we feel the effects half the world away. In addition, the concept of interconnectedness spans traditional spiritual and religious teachings as well as secular laws that promote ethical behavior. After all, each of us is simultaneously an individual and a member of a larger community.

By drawing the students' attention to this, you emphasize

the message that mindfulness of self and mindfulness of others are mutually reinforcing. From this point, you can empower students to recognize the importance of each person's position within the vast web of relationships. Class discussions about kindness and compassion feel more relevant to students when you consider the big picture while validating the individual's role. The point is to help students reflect that it's not just a question of whether *I experience more or less kindness*, but *how the quality of my actions impacts others*.

Defining Kindness

Before asking students to notice acts of kindness, it's a good idea to hold a brainstorming session to reach a shared definition of what they're looking for. Ask students to offer examples. Suggestions typically range from the profound, such as comforting a grieving friend, to the seemingly superficial, such as opening a door for a stranger. What's important is the recognition that kindness, as a quality, is present in many different situations. It's defining characteristic is the intention to express kindness and not the magnitude of the act.

Depending on your students' maturity and your time considerations, you might move on to a longer class discussion or simply remind students of the assignment and carry on with other activities. Should you wish to engage students in a more involved discussion on kindness, you might invite their responses to the idea that kindness relates more to the intention that infuses action rather than the actual action itself. Discuss whether there is a difference between doing something to highlight your kindness and acting with authentic kindness. You might also examine whether there is a difference between kindness associated with telling someone an uncomfortable truth and kindness that might prompt keeping that truth a secret.

Middle and high school students tend to recognize that simple formulae (or definitions) don't automatically define acts of kindness. They know appearances can be misleading. Genuine kindness can underlie apparently harsh actions. In contrast, a false veneer of kindness might be a cover for the opposite. Even elementary students are familiar with the basic concept and relate to examples from literature, fairy tales, and real life. For example, the gift of the red apple in Snow White teaches children to watch for similar enticements.

These are weighty issues that can be challenging for both students and teachers. If your students are ready to examine such topics, they will direct the discussion accordingly. If they don't naturally go in that direction, it's best to follow their lead and leave the deeper issues for another time. Bringing mindfulness to the discussion is important, no matter how the issues develop. Allowing for silence and time for processing buttresses the work you've put into building critical boundaries for safe space. Knowing when and how to intervene and redirect the discussion before students lose focus and/or confidence reinforces that trust as well.

There is a big difference between deep discussions appropriate for mainstream classrooms and the kind of therapeutic group processing found in the counselor's office. As the teacher, you'll need to enforce your regular ground rules so students feel comfortable engaging with complex and relevant issues without reaching an unproductive intensity. With careful attention and awareness, you'll know when you need to step in and bring students back to safe, familiar ground.

One way to bring them back is by making time for closure when ending the discussion. You might ask students to take a few mindful breaths or listen to the sound of the chime diminishing into silence. Or encourage them to notice, silently and privately, what they're feeling and thinking. Do they feel physically at ease, or do they notice tension or tightness in their bodies? If comfortable and appropriate in your class, you might also invite them to share their responses either verbally or in writing.

Should the class discussion cover challenging and sensitive ground, I strongly encourage you to end the discussion by reinforcing the students' sense of perspective and security. I tend to use a two-part message, but you can adapt or adopt these words as you see fit. First, I affirm that a discussion about kindness can lead to complex, and sometimes uncomfortable, issues and questions. The second part of the message is that most of us are nonetheless able to recognize our own—and others'—acts of kindness accurately, at least most of the time.

Most likely, students will realize authentic kindness feels good—both for the person acting with kindness and the recipient of it. Some will find this connection surprising whereas others will recognize the lesson as confirming what they already know from home, school, or involvement in community activities.

Managing other Emotions

Kindness is generally desirable, so increasing mindfulness of it seems doubly positive. But what happens when increased mindfulness of emotion leads to a greater awareness of less comfortable or welcome feelings such as envy or aggression? Applying mindfulness in these situations is still valuable, but in a different way.

Purposefully cultivating mindfulness of aggression, our own and that of others, is useful because we can become more skillful at working with the energy associated with aggression. That's very different from cultivating awareness of aggression in order to bring more aggression into the world. Similarly, cultivating mindfulness of envy to increase our skill in handling it is beneficial, the opposite of cultivating mindfulness of envy in order to fan its flames.

Applying mindfulness to feelings of aggression, envy, malice, or other strong—and often unconstructive—emotions strengthens the skills associated with managing them. Noticing their presence does not automatically increase the force of these emotions. Increased sensitivity to the presence of emotion boosts your ability either to reinforce or weaken its power. Just as noticing acts of kindness supports nurturing kindness, recognizing envy is the key to responding constructively when envy arises.

Mindfulness techniques are value-neutral because they support *noticing* not *judging*. Your attitude or orientation toward different emotions or qualities affects what you do after you notice them. Mindfulness enhances effective emotion management. It also promotes social and emotional skills, often initiating a cascade of desirable outcomes. Cultivating kindness can prompt inner compassion as well as the recognition and expression of compassionate acts toward others. This, in turn, helps relieve pain and supports happiness.

CHAPTER 6
Beads on a String

The trouble with meditation was that it was harder to talk about it than it was to do....

Tamora Pierce, *Cold Fire*

CONSIDER A STRING OF BEADS. We can regard each element in the day—waking up, commuting, greeting students, teaching lessons, going home—as akin to beads. And we can regard awareness as the string that holds each of the beads together (even though in any moment awareness may wax or wane in clarity). Mindfulness strengthens the string and also promotes resilience when the string drops. This chapter offers some tricks of the beader's trade that apply to teaching.

Mini Mindfulness Breaks

Whenever you pause spontaneously, to breathe and rest, you create spaces between the events of the day. These tiny rest spaces cue your attention to focus, again and again, on what's happening *now*. Just as you might use Take 5 before the students come into class, or Take 1 with students during class, you can also take a mini mindful breathing break, privately, in the midst of class. Any gap in the class's action—while students ponder a question, complete an equation, or even clean up—provides an opportunity for you to recenter in the midst of your own action. You can also pause during planning periods, recess or lunch duty, and even assemblies/announcements (so long as you're not in charge, of course).

Pausing in the midst of solving a problem is also valuable. Sometimes, one or more mindful breaths provide the mental energy and space for your mind to find a solution. Taking a brief rest allows the mind time to process new information, enhancing learning and memory. Pausing at the end of a task also promotes mental closure and gives you a chance to rest prior to focusing on the next activity.

This inner pause for a breath is usually invisible to everyone else. I'm not suggesting you close your eyes and zone-out or rest long enough for students to get curious. You'll still be alert to what's happening around you. In fact, you might even be more alert as a result of taking time to stop and notice. Rather than disrupting the flow of any activity, these mini mindfulness breaks contribute to continuity and coherence.

This suggestion for teaching mindfully, like some of the other ones we've explored, is really quite simple. Ironically, if they weren't quite so simple, and so obvious, they might be easier to remember to do and perhaps lead to fewer instinctive doubts. Maybe you wonder whether pausing for thirty seconds mid-class is of any real use? After all, it's so easy, and you might think, "How can anything this basic make any difference?" I've found such pauses work very powerfully, but the only way you'll know for sure is through your own experience of setting aside thirty-second intervals to calm the mind. The effects grow with repetition, but the immediate experience of taking such a brief rest is also beneficial.

Mindfulness Boosters and "Time In"

In addition to Take 1, there are many other techniques that provide mini mindfulness breaks. Not only do they allow you to calm the mind and catch up, but they also help to reinforce your regular mindfulness practice. These *mindfulness boosters* give your students and you "Time In"—time to check in with yourself—to refocus awareness and attention. These boosters require very little time because they build on the skills that develop through ongoing mindfulness training. Frequency of practice, far more than duration, primarily determines boosters' impact.

Although thinking about boosters provides context and intellectual motivation, the power of the practice comes from taking a momentary break from thinking. The basic methodology involves consciously and temporarily switching your attention from its current focus onto something else and then back again. Mindfulness boosters re-energize personal creativity and refine attention, rather than interrupting them. The following strategies can effectively catalyze attention and stimulate "Time In" for students of all ages. Choose the one that suits you best, or experiment with them all.

EXAMPLES OF "TIME IN"

- Ask for thirty seconds of silence in the middle of a lively class during which students stop reading, put down their pens, and simply take a brain rest. Then continue with the lesson.

- Ask students to focus their attention on the experience of opening and closing their hands. Then encourage them to give themselves a brief hand massage and feel the sensations in their hands.
- Invite students to listen to the ambient sounds in the room for thirty seconds without making any new sounds themselves.
- Suggest everyone stand up and flex their feet rising up onto tippy-toes, and then bring their soles flat to the ground, attending to the feelings in their feet and legs. Repeat several times.
- Draw the class's attention to a peaceful picture or poster in the room, and take a moment just to look at it.
- Play a one-minute clip of music—something calming, or focusing, or inspiring—and take a moment simply to listen.
- Ask students to take a breath and then release the breath as fast as possible, then take another and release it as slowly as possible. Then have them take a few mindful breaths before returning their attention to class.
- Suggest students stand up and walk three steps forward as slowly as possible while noticing how their feet feel on the floor and how other parts of their bodies move. Then ask them to walk backward, slowly and safely, to return to their desks, and sit down placing their awareness on the transition from movement to stillness.

Each of these techniques provides students with a brief opportunity to shift their attention away from academics and become aware of some other aspect of their current experience. Doing so facilitates calming—or organizing—their minds so they can shift back to learning with improved focus.

Boosters are most successful with elementary and middle school students if you simply implement the techniques and return to your regular curricular activities with little, if any, discussion. The students will welcome the break, and they probably won't really want, or need, to process the underlying concepts very much. Young students can benefit from participating even if they lack the developmental maturity necessary to discuss the quality of their experience.

Follow-up discussion becomes more important for high school students, and very mature eighth graders, especially as their thinking becomes more sophisticated. However, even with these students, including a visual component can boost communication because drawing a picture of an inherently non-verbal concept, such as the experience of calming the mind, is often easier than trying to find the right words.

For this next activity, each student will need a blank piece of paper, divided into three sections and at least one writing implement. However, it works best if students can work with different colored crayons, colored pencils, or markers. The following instructions offer an enhancement to Take 1 that provides students with an opportunity to describe their experience with a mindfulness booster graphically on paper:

DRAWING THE MIND: ENHANCEMENT FOR TAKE I (FOR STUDENTS)

Part I: Current Mental State

- Sit quietly. (Give students about thirty seconds before giving the next instruction.)
- Notice what's happening in your mind: are there thoughts, feelings, or sensations? None, some, or many? Do they remain the same or change?

- Draw a picture of your mental state right now in the left-hand third of your paper. (Give students a minute or so to complete their drawings.)
- Return to sitting quietly.
- Fold the left-hand third of the paper (with the drawing) face-down, so the two remaining blank sections remain face-up covering it.

Part 2: In Silence after the Sound

- Listen to the sound until it softens into silence. (Ring a note on your percussion instrument and wait until there is silence before giving the next instruction.)
- Notice what's happening in your mind now.
- Draw a picture of your mental state in the center third of your paper. (Give students a minute or so to complete their drawings.)
- Return to sitting quietly.
- Fold the center third of the paper (with the drawing) face-down, so now two sections are face-down toward the desk and only one blank section remains visible, face-up.

Part 3: Silence and Mindful Breathing

- Listen to the sound until it softens into silence. (Ring a note on your percussion instrument and wait until there is silence before giving the next instruction.)
- Switch your attention to noticing your breath.
- Breathe normally, paying attention to the feeling of the breath as it fills your lungs and then flows up and back out the way it came.

- Notice when you lose awareness of the breath and start thinking about something else, daydreaming, worrying, or snoozing.
- Bring your attention back to the breath.
- Notice what's happening in your mind now.
- Draw a picture of your mental state in the right-hand third of your paper. (Give students a minute to complete their drawings.)
- Return your awareness slowly to the classroom when you hear the sound marking the end of practice.
- Unfold the paper so the drawings in all three sections are visible.

The follow-up discussion for this booster is usually very short. Ask students to look at their drawings and reflect on their experiences. Invite a few volunteers to use their drawings and words to describe their mental state during the three parts of the activity. The most important comparison concerns students' experiences in Part 1 and Part 2—in other words, was there a difference in the students' mental state after simply sitting quietly without focusing on anything in particular, as compared to when they focused on listening to the diminishing sound? In addition, were there any differences in their mental state between Part 2 and Part 3? Ask students whether they can draw any conclusions, based on their own experiences, about the effects of mindfulness practice on mental state, and if so, what?

From your perspective, as the teacher, it's interesting to note privately whether the students' drawings are more, or less, informative than their verbal descriptions. Assuming students have a reasonable level of skill in drawing and verbal expression, the comparison between the two forms of communication can yield information relevant to other learning experiences. If students are able to draw their experience more precisely than their verbal articulation allows, you can incorporate drawing when checking for their understanding about social and emotional learning. In contrast, you can encourage students who write eloquently to try other forms of artistic expression.

Just as there are many extensions to this specific technique, there are endless variations to mindfulness boosters in general. I encourage you to try different approaches and invite your students to develop their own appropriate, time-limited techniques to share with the class. Also, gently push them to recognize *when* they need to rest so you can provide appropriate opportunities. Every time you use a booster, you'll increase your students' familiarity and confidence with the technique.

Mindful Eating

While eating is essential for physical survival, eating mindfully is about the quality of living in the moment. At school, the need for speed often pervades mealtimes so much you're likely to notice you already ate instead of realizing you are eating. The same holds true for students, and lunchrooms are rarely conducive to applying mindfulness to eating—at least, not when you're beginning the practice. Instead, serving a "snack" in class provides a more constructive opportunity for mindful eating, and teaching students to do so as well.

In the elementary grades, snack is a standard part of the schedule. Even though the official "snack time" disappears by middle and high school, older students enjoy food treats as well. As you'll see from the following instructions, the core progression to introducing mindfulness of taste and eating are very simple. The variations, however, are infinite.

The first basic step is to provide bite-sized inexpensive edible treats such as thin pretzels, cereal pieces, soft chocolates, or raisins. You'll need enough treats to distribute several pieces per student—with the understanding that students should not eat anything until you give the cue. With younger students or for safety reasons, you may want to pick foods that are harmless if accidentally swallowed without chewing—in other words, no whole grapes, caramels, or other potential hazards.

Once the students have the treats, invite them to eat one piece. The idea is to allow them to consume the first treat in their normal manner. Doing so provides a reference point for the next steps outlined below (each step can last around fifteen to sixty seconds, or can be varied as suits you):

MINDFUL EATING (FOR STUDENTS)

- Pick up another edible treat.
- Look at it closely and smell it.
- Place the treat in your mouth without chewing it.
- Become familiar with the treat in your mouth—how does it taste and feel?
- Pay attention to the experience of chewing and swallowing.
- Notice the aftertaste and any other sensations in your mouth that follow swallowing.
- Return your attention to the classroom.

At this point, invite the students to make a mental comparison between their experience eating the first treat (in their normal manner) and eating the second one mindfully. Then engage them in a discussion about the two experiences, asking for their observations. Students' responses can vary tremendously. Some will relish the experience of mindful eating. Others may dismiss the activity, almost on principle, and comment, "If you always ate that slowly you'd never have time to do anything else!"

Their skepticism is important, and it provides you with an opportunity to explain how mindfulness is relevant even though no one eats *that slowly* all the time. Slowing down artificially is simply a technique that fosters fresh experience within a routine activity. Since eating is so familiar, you need to employ something as extreme as radically changing the pace in order to focus students' attention. The idea is not to eat that slowly all the time, or even very often, but to do so from time to time just to rekindle awareness.

On a daily basis, mindful eating means noticing the process of eating, whether or not you slow down the pace of your meals. As with noticing thoughts, the emphasis is on watching what happens without engaging in actual content. So, too, with eating—the point is to cultivate an awareness of the experience without judging the specific characteristics.

Now, take a quick break from the analysis and invite your students to consume their last treat. Once they've done so, ask whether they enjoyed the third one more or less than the first (when they ate normally), and the second (when they ate very slowly).

Guide a discussion to examine how mindfulness—and its opposite, distraction—affects other aspects of the experience of eating. Your students have probably already had the experience of eating larger than normal quantities of salty and sweet snacks while watching an engaging movie. Most likely, they've noticed that the taste of salty and sweet foods naturally triggers the desire for more. But they might not have realized that placing their attention fully on the movie reduces the likelihood that they'll notice their body's cues indicating a full stomach and satisfaction.

It's important to be very clear that there is no inherent problem with eating sweet and salty snacks in moderation. They usually taste good, and applying mindfulness to eating can increase the enjoyment of savoring them. The issue is that, absent mindfulness, it's easy to eat too much and suffer the consequences. Similarly, eating a big meal can feel wonderful when you're hungry and noticing the sensation of filling your belly enhances the satisfaction. It also cues you to stop before you risk the discomfort associated with overeating.

Although mindful eating can enhance pleasure, it can also increase your awareness of unpleasant eating experiences. If you attend to *something you don't like eating*, you'll be more aware of your distaste. As a result, you might have an even stronger motivation to stop eating, or if you "have to" eat, you'll do so with the full knowledge that you are eating out of necessity and not for enjoyment.

Well-intentioned adults often tell kids to eat "healthy" foods including things they don't like. Occasionally, the unpleasantness of the situation leads to a disproportionately strong reaction. So, rather than avoiding just one kind of vegetable (because they hate it), they might shy away from all similar vegetables (because they must presumably taste the same) and maybe miss out on the opportunity to reclaim some vegetables that they could actually enjoy.

Ask your students if they're familiar with this type of situation. Then explore how applying mindfulness can help them regain the power to decide what they do and do not like to eat. Encourage them to choose what they want to eat based on their direct experience of eating and without the taint of past exposure. If they can distinguish between hating the taste of a specific food and disliking the order to eat it (and as a result deciding never to eat anything like that on principle), they'll have more power to choose what they want to eat *for themselves.*

Feed Your Mind

Although a mindful eating activity is likely to provoke an "a-ha" moment, there are many other less spectacular and more frequent opportunities for paying attention to *how* you eat and drink, along with *what* and *when* you do so. Beginning with your morning beverage, you can take the opportunity to enjoy the sensation of drinking as well as the psychological associations you attach to the experience. I like tea or coffee first thing. I love the taste, the heat, and the sensation of quenching my thirst. I also appreciate knowing I'll begin to feel more awake after I've sipped the first half cup. It's reassuring to know that I'll get less fuzzy when the cup is empty. I suspect I'm not alone in this experience.

The challenge is to cultivate the same appreciation for the experience of eating and drinking during the day. How does the water feel as you sip from the bottle on your desk? What does your lunch taste like? Is it delicious? If not, how does it taste? Rather than focusing on your response to or opinion of the taste, first pay attention to *the noticing* of the taste and then watch your response.

I'm not suggesting you purposefully eat things you don't like—rather I'm encouraging you to begin by noticing the taste before you name it. It's like realizing "Oh, this is crunchy, salty, and sort of sticky" before you attach the label "peanut butter" and the reaction "I love/hate crunchy peanut butter" to the substance in your mouth.

You can eat mindfully in silence or in the midst of a heated conversation. How you do so is personal and can be invisible. It's not necessary to chew so purposefully that everyone wonders what's wrong, or gaze off into the distance to savor a taste. Mindful eating is about setting an intention and then acting accordingly. It doesn't necessarily need to slow you down (although it might), but if you're gulping down lunch you'll know what you're doing *when you're doing it.*

Mindful meals can include eating as well as socializing or enjoying solitude. Sometimes you might need to be alone. On other days, you might gain energy by visiting with colleagues or students. Notice what you need, and then make choices that help you get what you need.

Mindfulness and Resilience

Mindfulness supports resilience, the ability to respond constructively to life. The ups and downs are inevitable. The challenge is to know how to re-center after falling off balance—and eventually, how to maintain balance in increasingly challenging situations. This applies to the big challenges, like losing a loved one, surviving an accident when others didn't, losing a job or home, or facing a serious illness. It also applies to smaller challenges that, nonetheless, affect a teacher's daily experience including:

- Watching students misbehave and feeling ineffective when you try to intervene.
- Getting chewed-out by your principal when you feel you didn't deserve it.
- Having to cover (again) for a colleague who shirks responsibilities.

The same applies to students. Changing schools, trouble at home, or feeling isolated from peers can be huge stressors. The smaller challenges can also be intense and disruptive. These might relate to:

- Feeling anxious before a test.
- Being left out of social cliques.
- Experiencing frustration and anger when learning is difficult or a teacher doesn't seem to understand the student's concerns.

Resilience is useful, whether the challenge is small and transitory, or life-changing and long-lasting. Learning how to promote resilience is important for your students—and for you. Mindfulness can feed resilience in four main ways that involve: (1) sensitivity, (2) self-calming, (3) managing suffering, and (4) recovering.

To begin with, mindfulness increases the sensitivity necessary to notice challenges. That is useful because the sooner you know you're facing something stressful, the more time you have to prepare and respond. Typically more options are available at the beginning of a sequence of events. The longer it takes to notice a problem, the greater the corresponding degree of effort required for an effective response. Simply put, mindfulness helps you see "it" coming earlier—whatever the "it" happens to be.

Secondly, mindfulness provides the training and practice necessary to develop skills to calm yourself. At first, you learn techniques, like watching the breath, that focus attention on the present moment. After practicing these techniques in a supportive environment, you can begin to apply them in real life. With time, you'll internalize the process of cultivating mindfulness in the midst of your daily activities. That means you'll be better able to practice self-calming, when needed. Eventually, the practice becomes automatic, and almost effortless.

Another part of self-calming concerns slowing down your habitual reactions to certain types of situations. Habitual reactions are the familiar thoughts and emotional patterns triggered by specific cues. The cues relate to past situations and cause you to remember the related thoughts and emotions. As you access these memories, you can benefit from past experience (you don't need to repeat a faulty experiment to prove that it doesn't work), but you can also burden your present with unconstructive baggage (you don't need to assume that something is really wrong every time your principal asks to see you, even though there has been something wrong the last two times you had a meeting).

Unnoticed habitual reactions, even when based on valid past experiences, can nonetheless lead to an inappropriate response given current conditions. For example, if you felt angry when criticized in the past, you might be quick to anger as soon as you perceive criticism. Intense anger, shutting down emotionally, and negative thoughts are common habitual patterns.

These habits are learned over a lifetime. Initially, most of them served a purpose and helped you to cope with a difficult situation. When you repeat these responses over and over again, you train the mind to react to specific types of situations in a particular, familiar manner. This simple cause and effect system explains how you develop constructive as well as unconstructive patterns over time. The more you repeat a pattern, the more automatic it becomes. In this way, the past informs the present and the future.

As with the body's physiological response to physical threats, emotions arise faster than thoughts. So when something happens to trigger a familiar emotional pattern, you feel your response before you have had a chance to think about whether the response is warranted. Mindfulness trains you to slow down and notice what's really happening, and therefore lets your thoughts catch up with your feelings to promote a balanced response. This is at the heart of resilience.

The third way mindfulness supports resilience concerns how you manage emotional and physical suffering—from low-level discomfort to intense trauma. By practicing mindfulness of emotion and physical sensation, you learn to notice an experience without fully engaging in it. Mindfulness is not about denial or dismissing pain. Rather, it is about directly experiencing comfortable and uncomfortable emotions and sensations as constructively as possible.

The act of witnessing is important. It allows you to recognize pain, feel pain, and still know you are somehow more than that pain. Some part of consciousness simultaneously experiences being aware and being aware of whatever is happening. You can feel pain and know the pain does not fully define you. This perspective facilitates dealing with reality. It also helps you recover from an intense experience, because you can see that things and experiences change over time. In other words, sometimes life is really difficult, and you know that you hurt—and not just a little. At the same time, some part of the mind recognizes you also have the capacity to find life beautiful and rejoice.

Recovering after facing a challenge is the fourth area in which mindfulness provides support. The aim here is to develop the skills to re-center as easily and quickly as possible so you can move on. Although it's healthy to process your experiences, in order to learn from them, many people tend to replay the past in ways that prolong the pain. That kind of reliving is not constructive, and, at the brain level, weakens well-being by reinforcing suffering.

Noticing when you are reliving the past is the first step toward shifting your attention to the present. Mindfulness facilitates this step. It also facilitates the act of remembering to shift attention to the present *without self-judgment or inner commentary.*

Mindfulness of Thoughts for Students

Rapidly changing thoughts and emotions provide a dynamic context for exercising resilience. Mindfulness helps develop a resilient response to challenges and this includes noticing inner cues for doing so. One of the more important skills involves distinguishing between *the transient experience* of a thought or feeling and *the acceptance* of that thought or feeling as a solid fact. Mindfulness of thought is the basis for developing this skill—for your students and for you.

With elementary and middle school students, it's often best to discuss the subject of mindful thinking within the framework of a more tangible activity such as mindful seeing, listening, or tasting. Younger students tend to associate their thoughts (and thought processes) with the "self" and too much direct emphasis on "watching thoughts" can confuse them. Asking them to focus on mindful breathing and to notice when they are distracted draws their attention to thoughts in a roundabout way. This works precisely because you help them pay attention to their experience directly, and sidestep the abstract issues like "How can I think about thinking" or "I am thinking, so who is there to watch that thinking?"

In contrast, most high school students have the mental maturity to distinguish between noticing thoughts and *thinking about thinking*. Introducing them to a simple Mindful Thinking progression provides a framework that helps them watch how thoughts arise and dissolve and reminds them to refrain from following storylines. Lead into this progression by practicing mindful breathing for a few minutes, and then guide students through the following steps:

NOTICING THOUGHTS (FOR STUDENTS)

- Breathe normally, paying attention to the feeling of the breath as it fills your lungs and then flows up and back out the way it came.
- Notice when a thought arises.
- Acknowledge the thought, perhaps by saying "thinking" silently in your mind.
- Switch your attention from that thought in particular, back to watching for thoughts in general.
- Continue watching and acknowledging thoughts until your session ends.
- Be patient, gentle, and kind with yourself.

Follow up with a discussion after using Noticing Thoughts with high school students. See if they are intrigued by the difference between watchful and analytical awareness and if they can discern the presence of thoughts and the spaces between the thoughts. The gaps between thoughts are alert pauses—there's a sense of presence but no conscious separation from that sense. The thought "Oh, that's a space between thoughts" comes later, once the gap closes.

Gaps, like thoughts, come and go. There's no need to force them or celebrate them—they're simply part of the mind's natural experience. If students demonstrate interest in noticing the gaps, try the following progression, but let them know this version can be quite challenging:

NOTICING GAPS (FOR STUDENTS)

- Breathe normally, paying attention to the feeling of the breath as it fills your lungs and then flows up and back out the way it came.
- Notice when a thought arises.
- Acknowledge the thought, perhaps by saying "thinking" silently in your mind.
- Switch your attention back to watching for thoughts in general.
- Notice whether there is any space between switching your attention from inwardly acknowledging a thought or saying "thinking" to watching for the next thought, and then let the space go without labeling it.
- Continue watching thoughts and gaps until your session ends.
- Be patient, gentle, and kind with yourself.

Some students are likely to "get it" immediately, but the majority are more than likely to feel confused or frustrated while trying to focus on the spaces between thoughts. Reassure everyone that the effort is what's important, whether or not they notice the gaps or feel annoyed and angry. If they don't find any gaps, that is fine and they are not "missing something." Their confusion and frustration are normal, and actually provide another opportunity for them to apply mindfulness to noticing how feelings come and go.

Since most students find this technique sufficiently challenging, it's probably best simply to work with the label "thoughts" as a catch-all for all mental events, emotional feelings, and physical sensations. By contrast, Chapter 2 presented a progression for noticing emotions, for your use. Those instructions are also appropriate for mature high school students, but there's no need to introduce that added level of refinement unless your students indicate they want to explore other approaches.

You can take a discussion of mindful thinking one step further when you have a group of high school students eager to learn more about mindfulness. To do so, alternate between mindfulness practice and an analytical discussion that explores the differences between "thoughts" and "attention"—experientially and intellectually. Ask students to define the terms. Eventually ask them if they are willing to accept working definitions that "thoughts are mental events" and attention is a "quality of focus." If so, continue, and if not, find acceptable alternatives. Then ask students, "Is it possible to think without paying attention to thinking?" Can they pay attention to thoughts as well as the pauses in between? Discuss their responses, and then consider whether recognizing the pauses can lead people to develop a different relationship with their thoughts.

In the past, you might have assumed your thoughts somehow reflected the "true" you. Once you notice that you experience thoughts much the same way as you experience physical sensations or emotions, you might relate to your thoughts with more openness. This doesn't mean your thoughts aren't important, it's just that you are more than your thoughts and thoughts are not themselves ultimate truths.

Thinking in Class

Helping students realize they can notice their thoughts has practical benefits for their classroom behavior. Respecting other people's thoughts might become easier for students who know, through experience, that thoughts are personal mental events, and not necessarily objective reality. In other words, "I have my thoughts" and "you have your thoughts" in precisely the same way. By extension, if I disagree with your thoughts, I can notice that "I" disagree. And, whether or not I agree with the content of your thoughts, I affirm that you have your thoughts.

Mindful thinking can also help you recognize the difference between disagreeing with someone's thoughts and judging the person as a whole. This is an expansion on the conventional practice of focusing on the behavior rather than the person (i.e., "I don't like how you lied to me yesterday about..." vs. "you are a liar"). Many teachers model this approach regularly as a best practice. Highlighting the role of mindfulness simply enriches the lesson.

As students mature developmentally, the distinction between action and person, or thought and person, becomes easier to understand and accept. Developing mindfulness of thought assists this process. The main idea is to guide students to recognize the value of thoughts (as well as emotions and sensations) while maintaining the perspective that the nature of thoughts, emotions, and sensations is personal and dynamic. Although thoughts, emotions, or sensations define an individual's moment-to-moment experience, there is more to each person than what he or she does, feels, or thinks at any given moment.

This realization can help students accept critical feedback on their work. They are more willing to stretch academically when they realize they are "okay" even when they get an answer wrong. The logic of this situation is simple: "If I am not (only) my thoughts, then I can experiment with different thoughts—and make mistakes—without somehow risking my identity or integrity." Such intellectual openness, combined with empathy, is among the roots of tolerance for oneself and others. Academically, these qualities are among those most essential for intellectual engagement and mastery.

CHAPTER 7
Body Awareness

"But this is meditating, only we're moving," she panted, bracing her hands on her knees. She felt wonderful.

"That's all it should be. I never could sit on my behind and count myself silly," Skyfire replied breathlessly. "I meditate this way."

Tamora Pierce, *Cold Fire*

THE PHYSICAL EXPERIENCES of movement and the physical experience of stillness are like two sides of the same coin. They are interconnected, just as paying attention and developing the awareness of paying attention; each contains the essence of the other. As long as you are alive, there is always movement within your body, even when you are outwardly absolutely still. At the same time, it is possible to find an awareness of stillness even in the midst of intense and hurried movement. Runners find this mental stillness when they enter "the zone," as do dancers, other athletes, and performing artists. With mindfulness practice you can also learn to access this experience when you are in the midst of teaching.

You can, for instance, briefly apply mindfulness to your felt awareness as well as your mental and emotional responses. What is your body telling you about this situation? Are you standing still, in shock, or moving with nervousness? If you're standing "still," attend to the subtle movements within you, noticing the presence (or absence) of tightening muscles, a clenching jaw, or a racing heart. Consider whether your felt awareness is sending signals that jive with your thoughts about the situation and your feelings. If your experiences are consistent, then you're in a clear position. If not, it might be good to examine the discrepancy.

Accurately interpreting other people's words is another benefit of applying mindfulness to body, speech (as in their delivery), and thoughts (in this case, meaning the words they choose). This has been tremendously helpful to me when a student's facial expression, word-choice, or gestures somehow communicate distress or unusual discomfort in the midst of a class on HIV prevention. When I see these clues, I need to follow up with the student in an appropriate setting after class. My observations in class combined with the discordance between a student's assertion "everything is fine" and his shaky voice and averted eyes indicate the need for follow-up.

A discrepancy among verbal and non-verbal messages doesn't always foretell a crisis or significant situation. Sometimes, it's simply a result of distraction or fatigue. It's easy to miss the messages of felt awareness because they're often subtle, like the warmth that rises in your face from pleasure, the mild tightness in your throat that indicates nervousness, or the shortness in your speech that suggests impending exhaustion.

There's often something to learn when your statement, "Everything is fine," receives the reply, "You don't look like everything is fine." In this case, another person's observation of a disconnect between your words and your presentation can serve as a timely reminder to check-in with yourself and make sure everything really is fine. The body knows, and almost always shows, what's really happening, and practicing mindfulness increases sensitivity to recognizing these signals.

Cultivating Felt Awareness for Yourself

There are many informal and formal ways to apply mindfulness to physical sensations and movement. Informal methods infuse daily experience with mindfulness, whereas formal techniques employ dedicated practice with specific techniques. Informal techniques grow organically within the context of normal activity, whereas formal techniques introduce a particular format that emphasizes certain outcomes. Both are valuable and complementary, so the challenge is to sequence them constructively.

Beginning with a formal practice is advisable because doing so offers optimal conditions for paying attention to sensations and movement. Techniques involving a Body Scan are among the most common approaches that train awareness on physical sensation. Preparation for a Body Scan is simple. Initially, you'll need ten to twenty minutes in which to lie quietly on the floor or sit still in a chair, preferably with your back comfortably supported and straight. As you gain familiarity with the technique, you'll be able to apply it effectively in briefer stretches of time.

Begin by focusing your awareness on your feet and then, one body-area at a time, move your attention from your lower extremities, to your abdomen, toward your neck, then from your hands inward toward the shoulders, and finally from your neck up to the crown of the head. You deepen your awareness of physical sensation sequentially, working with the parts and eventually resting in the experience of the body as a whole. The purpose of this activity is to "check in" with each part of your body, to enhance your physical self-awareness. Some people find it fruitful to follow the Body Scan with what is called "progressive muscle relaxation," in which you gradually tense then relax each muscle group.

The Body Scan promotes attention to normal sensations in the body as well as unusual feelings. In daily life, it's often easy to overlook the experience of normal feelings—precisely because *they're ordinary and fine.* By contrast, something "atypical" demands attention. As a result, noticing the extremes—of pain or pleasure—takes precedence and eventually becomes habitual. That's fine unless experiencing the extremes feels more normal (and desirable) than sustainable ordinary experience. Cultivating mindfulness of all sensations helps avoid that situation by training the mind to notice without automatically dismissing the "normalness" of ordinary experience.

Although you can certainly use the Body Scan methodology to develop awareness in the midst of movement, beginning with stillness is important because the absence of outer movement reduces distraction. Nevertheless, the Body Scan is essentially about maintaining awareness and attention while noticing the sensations within the body. Conducting a Body Scan often provides a powerful, highly personal experience. You might find the process alternately relaxing, challenging, uncomfortable, or surprising—physically, mentally, and emotionally.

The individual and unpredictable nature of the Body Scan experience is precisely the reason why I suggest you use this technique, yourself, at home or in other safe places, and caution against school-based use. Not only is the school environment too public and distracting, but more importantly, few teachers have the psychological training to respond effectively should a student experience a flashback of trauma during a Body Scan in class. The risk is significant and the responsibilities heavy should a student have this type of reaction. Fortunately, as you'll see in the next sections, there are other appropriate and effective techniques for use with students.

First, let's return to the subject of developing mindfulness of sensation and movement for yourself. Once you've developed a basic familiarity with this application of mindfulness through working with a formal technique like the Body Scan, you are ready to begin using informal techniques in dynamic situations like listening to a student's unexpected outburst. As previously described, the first step is to cultivate mindfulness and notice what's happening in and around you.

The second step involves taking quick action internally based on the awareness you've just cultivated. So, if you notice your body is suddenly tight and your stance feels rigid, inhale and sharpen focus on your posture. Then, as you exhale, consciously guide your body to permit greater flexibility and movement. This might mean you pay attention to relaxing and lengthening, envisioning your body full of energy, or make an adjustment that feels right to you. This simple, brief technique occurs quickly—in the space of one breath.

Once you've done this, return your attention to the student and your classroom. The physical results of this technique can be very subtle, even invisible, to the class. However, the mental and emotional benefits will inform the quality of your presence in the room. The constructive ripple effects are potentially enormous. Even if this technique simply provides a tiny respite in which to center yourself, your increased stability will permeate your response.

The opportunities for developing mindfulness of sensation and movement through applying a combination of formal and informal techniques are endless. In addition, the sum of these two variables is somehow greater than the parts. Formal techniques hone focus on your body sensations and movements so that you bring greater skill to dynamic situations. Informal techniques provide relevant opportunities for practical application and practice of the attention and awareness skills developed through formal exercises. Over time, the back-and-forth cycle between formal practice and informal application reinforces and stabilizes the practice.

Mindful Movement with Students

Students benefit from formal mindful movement techniques and there are many appropriate methodologies from which to choose. Some are one-time-only activities like the Walking with Awareness or Mindful Movement techniques highlighted in this section. Others involve highly disciplined techniques that require ongoing practice such as yoga, martial arts, and Tai Chi typically only available as extracurricular activities or through a trained specialist.

If you have special training in these formal techniques, you could incorporate them in your classroom teaching. However, you might encounter parental or community resistance if you introduce yoga or other movement practices derived from Eastern traditions. If this seems likely in your situation, go slowly and be sure you have administrative and parental support. Even if you aren't in a position to share your training in these disciplines directly with students, remember that embodying mindfulness in the classroom is far more important than practicing any particular technique.

Walking with Awareness works as a basic introductory approach that engages students of all ages with the activity before even mentioning the term mindfulness. The instructions prompt students to walk in different ways that communicate and reflect their awareness of specified emotions, thoughts, and sensations. The idea is to build on the momentum related to students' familiarity with walking "as if" they're tired, proud, or procrastinating, to create an opportunity in which they focus on walking while attending only to the experience of walking. The activity works best when preceded by a short introduction that simply serves to arrange students in an open space in the classroom, followed by a discussion afterward. The instructions coach the students through the activity as follows:

WALKING WITH AWARENESS (FOR STUDENTS)

- Begin walking slowly within the open area in the classroom, silently and without bumping into others.
- Walk normally among each other, without following any pattern.
- Walk as if you're very tired.
- Walk as if you've just heard the most exciting, wonderful news.
- Walk as if your ankle hurts.
- Walk as if you think everyone is watching you.
- Walk as if you want to delay arriving somewhere.
- Walk as if you want to pass unnoticed in a crowd.
- Walk as if you feel proud.

- Walk as if you don't know where you are (or where you're going).
- Walk while paying attention to every movement you make with each step.

After completing the last task, ask students to return to their seats and invite them to comment on the activity. Ask them, "Why did we do this?" You may hear students offer responses like, "because how you walk shows other people what you're feeling inside," and "what you think and feel affects how you walk." The next step is to guide them to switch their focus to the interrelationships between body language, thoughts, feelings, and sensations. Explore the way past experience informs current experience by commenting on how they appeared to know just how to walk as if they felt tired, had a hurt ankle, or felt everyone else was watching them—even though they weren't necessarily experiencing any of those feelings in reality.

If you ask them to explain why they were able to walk so convincingly, they are likely to refer to times in the past when they walked while tired, hurt, or self-conscious. Then ask them how they knew how to "walk while paying attention to every movement" and expect diverse answers. Some students will repeat the earlier statement that they could do that because they already knew how. Others will say they were confused and didn't know what to do. Still others might say that they never paid attention to walking normally before, even though they've walked for years. Others might model walking very slowly. This part of the discussion provides a platform for introducing the concept of mindfulness as a purposeful focusing on experiencing whatever we naturally experience.

Another avenue for discussion involves exploring how the instruction to "walk while paying attention to every movement" differs from all the other directions to walk "as if." Ask students whether they could walk "while paying attention" to their feelings of happiness, anger, exhaustion, or any other experience. Since they have already demonstrated they can walk as if they embodied different experiences, inquire what—if anything—is different when they walk while actually living those experiences.

These are subtle questions, and it's impossible to predict the response of any given kindergarten to twelfth-grade student. Sometimes the youngest students actually offer answers that demonstrate greater clarity than the oldest. Whether it is a student or you who provides an answer, the point is very simple. Walking with mindfulness doesn't necessarily change your normal movements—it simply changes your experience of them. Even if some students don't understand the concept of mindful walking, they are still likely to benefit from getting up out of their chairs and participating in quiet, focused movement.

After introducing mindfulness, you can move to more specific explorations. While Walking with Awareness began with movement and then applied mindfulness, Mindful Walking begins with cultivating mindfulness before focusing on movement. This simple technique requires sufficient open space in the classroom to arrange pieces of easy-to-remove tape on the floor around the room. Mark three shapes with the tape: a straight line (about 10 feet long), a gently rounded half circle or "S" shape, and an interrupted line alternating pieces of tape (about a foot each) with spaces of the same length forming a "- - - -" sequence.

This technique is appropriate at all grade levels, however

it's important to consider the size and maturity of the class in deciding whether you work with them all together (beginning with the straight line), or divide them into three smaller groups and assign each to one of the three different taped patterns. As you'll see, the instructions are common to all the patterns, and students should try all three before any class discussion:

MINDFUL WALKING (FOR STUDENTS)

- Begin walking normally but very slowly while keeping your feet on the taped line.
- Make the smallest movements possible as you walk.
- Return your awareness to the experience of walking if you find yourself focusing on something else.
- Don't worry if you lose your balance and fall off the line, just pay attention while repositioning yourself and continue walking.

After everyone finishes walking on all three lines, hold a class discussion on the students' experience. Ask them to comment on paying attention to walking on each of the different shapes. How did they feel? Was it easy or difficult? Encourage them to explain why walking on the line leads to a different experience than simply walking slowly around the room. They are likely to point out, "No one walks that slowly." You can respond by saying the activity works precisely because that's true. Isolating the experience of walking, by artificially slowing it down through demanding greater precision, prompts students to focus more deeply and on smaller increments of movement than normal speeds allow. In addition, the extreme slowness creates the feeling of a distinct activity.

Another avenue for discussion involves exploring connections between movement and concentration. Ask students whether they felt focused or distracted when walking mindfully. Did walking on the lines help calm their minds or give them an opportunity to think about other things? Consider whether they ever use motion to help them focus on something else. For example, do they pace while memorizing, fiddle with their feet while working through a math problem, or twirl their hair while reading? If so, encourage them to brainstorm about opportunities for using movement mindfully to increase their focus in the classroom. Ask the students if they would like to experiment with taking brief mindful walking breaks during class, before tests, or when they're emotionally wound-up.

You can implement one or both of the following variations either after the class discussion, or better yet, on different days. While it's always important to follow the activity portion with a discussion, subsequent debriefs can be shorter than the initial one. Also, if students enjoy this activity, you can add other variations appropriate to their physical skill and maturity—and encourage them to create and introduce variations of their own. Here are two variations appropriate for middle and high school students:

MINDFUL WALKING—ATTENDING TO THE BODY (FOR STUDENTS)

(Use taped lines, or simply ask your class to walk slowly around the room since they are already familiar with the basic experience.)
- Begin walking normally, but very slowly (while keeping your feet on the taped line, if applicable).

- Notice the sensations in your feet, legs, torso, arms, neck, and head—do they feel relaxed, tight, heavy, flexible, or something else?
- Notice your breath—is it fast, slow, deep, or shallow, or are you holding your breath?
- Return your awareness to the experience of walking if you lose focus.
- Don't worry if you lose your balance (and fall off the line), just pay attention while repositioning yourself and continue walking.

MINDFUL WALKING—DEVELOPING AWARENESS WITH DISTRACTION (FOR STUDENTS)

(Use taped lines for this variation and arrange students in single file so they can follow each other *as closely as possible without touching*.)

- Begin walking normally but very slowly while keeping your feet on the taped line.
- Notice your own movements and sensations.
- Notice if/when you become aware of someone behind or in front of you on the line, and then return your attention to your own movement immediately.
- Return your awareness to the experience of walking if you lose focus.
- Don't worry if you lose your balance and fall off the line, just pay attention while repositioning yourself and continue walking.

Some students will naturally prefer developing mindfulness through movement, using Mindful Walking or similar techniques, instead of working with more sedentary practices like

Mindful Breathing. That's fine; it is important to encourage them to pursue whichever feels more helpful whenever they have the option to choose. However, remind them there are many life situations in which they will have no choice but to sit still, just as there are instances in which they will have no choice but to keep moving, and therefore learning how to practice mindfulness in both contexts is practical and valuable.

Mini Mindfulness Movement Techniques

Mini mindfulness movement techniques facilitate moving through the day with greater awareness and physical ease. Sometimes the school day feels like a marathon, and you might need lots of little breaks and changes of pace to reach the end on your feet. Other days, teaching classes seems like running sprints, and your body's demands for energy are different. Regardless of the nature of the day, briefly applying mindfulness to movement and sensation can make a significant difference to the quality of your experience.

Paying attention to your legs and feet when you walk into school first thing in the morning is a good place to begin. Consider whether your limbs feel light and energetic, heavy and tired, stable or wobbly as they move. Just notice without inner commentary or interpretation. Return to experiencing your sensations directly if you catch yourself basing assumptions about the future on your present experience. So, if you hear your inner voice complain, "I can't believe my legs are already dragging; it's going to be a really long day," just mentally nod to the thought, let it go, and return to feeling. On the other hand, if your legs feel heavy and tired, use that direct information as motivation to sit down as much as you can that day.

Your classroom provides another opportunity for attending to your physical experience while supervising students during standardized tests or exams. Notice the quality of your energy while walking up and down the aisles. Are you nervous, anxious, encouraged, or just curious about the test? If you recognize that you feel stress, focus your attention on walking mindfully and noticing the sensations of slow movement. As you switch your attention to mindful walking, your presence in the classroom is also likely to change. Your increased steadiness will sustain and encourage your students as they work, just as your increased focus prompts students' focus, and your calmness cues theirs. In this way, you can shift your experience with supervision so you ensure proper procedures while actively, and appropriately, supporting the students' performance.

The way you handle physical discomfort also impacts students' learning. Consider the implications related to lugging physically heavy things around school. If your experience of lifting, moving, and setting things down is acceptable, then carry on. But if the required exertion takes a toll on your energy or results in physical pain, then you need to make changes so as to minimize your burden. This is just one example illustrating the importance of attending to your experience and caring for yourself so you can focus all your energy on teaching your students.

Another example involves noticing your physical sensations while working at the computer. Focus on your hands, neck, and shoulders—are you comfortable and at ease? Or is there tension in your body? Does your chin jut up and out, putting pressure on your neck? Or do you tuck it down slightly to straighten your spine, like you do when practicing Take 5 or Take 1? Use your awareness to cue physical and mental breaks. If your wrists are rigid and stiff, take the time to flex your hands. If you feel sleepy or dull, re-energize by breathing some fresh air and moving around to increase oxygen flow. Punctuating work sessions with periods of gentle movement helps clear the mind and nurture the body.

Students also need to get up, move around, stretch, and breathe, in order to sustain their attention. Furthermore, they might need you to teach them how to notice and respond to the felt-awareness signals indicating their needs for breaks and mindfulness boosters. If they misinterpret or fail to recognize these messages, they are likely to lose focus without knowing why or what else to do. It's useful to know the body needs to release tension through movement to avoid discomfort and the distraction associated with it. Allowing students to learn this fact through experience is probably the most effective way to teach this particular lesson.

You can help students link felt-awareness with mental attention through an in-class experiment. In the midst of an intense academic lesson, stop and ask everyone to locate the big joint of the jaw. Do the same yourself. Then ask students whether they feel tension in their jaw and/or neck and head? If so, encourage them to use the information provided by this felt-awareness to guide action. Take a minute, mid-class, and invite students to massage, stretch, or move their jaws, necks, and heads. Then return to teaching. A few minutes later, ask them to notice how they feel and whether they are thinking more effectively, or less? How about you?

Attending to your jaw, carrying heavy objects, or walking among students taking an exam can be canvases onto which you apply simple techniques and blend the two main ideas behind mindful movement. The basic idea is to attend to your body's sensations and movement. That's the mindfulness part. The next step is practical application, which means that you merge your behavior and actions with your awareness to support physical and emotional health and well-being.

When Class Ends Before You're Done

Endings are just as important as beginnings, whether for an activity, class, or the school day—and greetings inevitably lead to partings. Although beginnings pose challenges, I tend to find endings more difficult. There's something ominous about the firm deadlines imposed by schedules. As a result, I've grown familiar with the experience of hearing the school bell ring midsentence and helplessly watching my students gather their belongings and rush off to their next class. If you're like me, you know how rotten this experience feels.

There you are, closing in on the end of the period realizing you're only midway through your lesson plan. It's tempting to push ahead and cover as much content as possible, but this risks leaving the class unfinished and ultimately sabotages learning. On the other hand, if you reconcile yourself to your position, and stop teaching new content in time to reinforce the main points you have a good shot at ending class satisfied. From this perspective, the measure of a successful class is not *how much material you covered*, but *how well the students learned*.

So, how do you bring mindfulness into that moment when class has to end and you're not ready? If you've been cultivating mindfulness formally and in less pressured situations (such as at home) you'll already have some familiarity with the experience of shifting your attention purposefully. It is time for informal practice; taking a breath and pausing for a few seconds marks the transition. During that brief time, notice your feelings and any self-talk. Do you feel frustrated, angry, or amused with yourself? Just notice, don't engage. Knowing what you're feeling before you say anything to the class will help you choose what you say and how you say it. The more inner calm you can muster at this crunch moment, the less pressured you will feel.

Next, acknowledge what's happened with a statement like, "Well, the time went by too fast and I haven't finished everything yet." Narrating the obvious is important because doing so models that you're fallible but flexible. Over time, as you become more mindful at the end of class, you'll remember to apply mindfulness earlier during your lesson. This improves your skill with assessing whether or not you will cover everything you have planned. From there, it's easier to make adjustments in your expectations and pacing to ensure you have enough time for a proper wrap-up.

For now, when time runs short, something has to give—either the amount of material you cover or the time you use to end the class, and you have to decide, on the spot, what's best for today. Perhaps you truly need to speed-talk through explaining the homework, or maybe you decide to postpone the assignment. Whenever possible, release students on time with a mindful "goodbye," and send them home without the stress of having an assignment they don't fully understand. Making time to explain assignments thoroughly communicates the value you place on their work and motivates them to work more seriously.

Even when the bell rings, you can still say goodbye sincerely. Farewells are as important as greetings. They can be quicker, but they are no less significant. Finish your sentence, look around the room, and tell your students you look forward to seeing them later or the next day. Communicate that *they* are more important to you than whatever point you were trying to make. The relationships come first, and strong connections between teacher and students create a solid basis for motivated learning.

Later in the day, try to reflect on the experience of running out of time and see what you could do differently in the future. Find one thing that might help and set the intention to try it. This could be shortening your lesson plan, checking the clock more often, or beginning the class by describing that night's homework assignment. Look at all your options and aim to use time more efficiently while promoting a healthy classroom climate. You may want to write a note to yourself so you don't forget your intention, and then focus on whatever is happening in the current moment.

If the first class of the day ends before you are ready to end it, you might find yourself rushing into the next class somewhat distracted. Rushing (and feeling rushed) tends to decrease attention. In contrast, staying present in the moment and adjusting your teaching as necessary can enhance attention—for your students and yourself. Proper endings allow for closure and decrease the chance that the experience of the previous class will influence the next one. Staying mindfully present is the lubricant that smoothes your movements as well as the transitions between and within classes.

Mindfully dismissing students at the end of the day initiates the last transition of the school day. Saying "goodbye" sincerely sends students out into the larger community grounded in a strong connection to school and to you as their teacher. Doing so also expresses your acknowledgement that both students and teachers have personal lives and relationships outside school. Bridging school and the outer community builds teacher-student interactions that nurture the "whole child." There is more to each individual student and teacher than the classroom, and validating the existence of a personal identity and home life is respectful and supportive of everyone.

CHAPTER 8
Mindful Words

Your mind needs discipline. If your thinking is more direct, what you can *do* with your thoughts will happen more directly. Learn to focus your mind: focus creates strength. Meditation helps you reach the same end.

Tamora Pierce, *Wild Magic*

THE TECHNIQUES EXPLORED so far all have the potential to influence the kinds of things you choose to say and the manner in which you choose to say them. But maintaining mindfulness in the course of a meaningful conversation can be a particular challenge. Dialogue involves a degree of mutual attention, or attunement, between participants. Even when people are highly attentive, the spontaneity and velocity of spoken language increase the risk of miscommunication. Also, the flow of conversation necessitates an instantaneous and accurate assessment of meaning on which to base the development and delivery of an appropriate response. Missing a cue in the speaker's tone, assumptions, or intentions can rapidly unravel the discourse. When you apply mindfulness to speech, you protect against this undesirable outcome as you develop skills for listening carefully and openly to other people's speech and concurrently cultivating greater awareness of your own.

Mindful speech is the goal, and you can help students pay attention to verbal expression through a variety of writing, reading, and speaking techniques in the classroom—before they purposefully apply mindfulness to real-time dialogue. Mindful writing involves applying awareness of thoughts and attention to written expression. Journaling enhances other mindfulness practices and reinforces reflections on kindness. Reading or listening to someone else read aloud complements mindful speech by providing the outside stimulus needed to focus attention on both listening and understanding another person's words. Whether you begin by applying mindfulness to writing and reading or to speaking and listening is a matter of personal preference.

Mindfulness Journals

Keeping a mindfulness journal differs from conventional journaling in several significant ways and it's helpful to try the process out for yourself, before implementing it with students. With mindfulness, journaling is about the experience of writing and awareness of recollection rather than narrative or analysis. If possible, you might try to carry the journal with you and write short entries in the midst, or shortly after, different experiences.

Unlike keeping a diary, mindful journaling avoids a comprehensive accounting of your time or a discourse on the meaning of past experiences. Mindful journaling works best if you write in the present tense, recording something like, "I see the coffee and cookies that come with faculty meetings and I feel hungry," rather than, "Earlier today, I felt hungry after I smelled the coffee and cookies." The difference between the two statements mostly relates to your position vis-à-vis your experience. You are part of the action in mindful journaling, whereas you write about the action in a conventional diary.

Mindful journaling also challenges you to use verbs in the first person. You write about your own experience, noticing what's happening as you have the experience. Stick with what you know, firsthand, and refrain from developing any third person commentary on other people's actions or perspectives. Also, while journaling, notice whether your attention stays with present (or recent) events or whether you are drawn into the tempting, and almost endless, "what ifs" of the past and future. Refraining from rehashing the past or continuously worrying about the future in your journal increases your sensitivity to staying present during conversation.

Journaling about your daily intentions first thing in the morning also heightens awareness of a particular quality or aim during the day. Writing again before bed facilitates further reflection on that intention. Similarly, setting the intention to write in school at mid-day and purposefully placing your journal on your desk supports follow-through. Linking writing with practicing other mindfulness techniques like Take 1, Take 5, or Mindful Walking further enhances your formal practice. All of these strategies share the common element of anchoring mental tasks (like setting intentions) to actual physical actions (such as writing about your intentions) to stabilize and sustain mindfulness.

Your students can also benefit from keeping their own mindfulness journals in class, especially if you participate in the activity along with them. Your direct modeling brings a sense of normalcy to journaling. After all, if you're willing to make the time to write, your students are likely to join you.

There are many, many ways to work with mindfulness and journaling in class. Trying different approaches with students makes sense and allows your class and you several opportunities to experiment and find the best fit. The preparation is typically simple and identical, regardless of journaling methodology. Students need a small, single-subject notebook or journal in which to work and you need to designate several minutes of class time during which they write.

Introducing Mindful Journaling as a lesson extension for Take 1 presents the journal format in a familiar context and simultaneously enhances the activity. The following instructions guide fifth- through twelfth-grade students to write something about their experience with Mindful Breathing:

MINDFUL JOURNALING WITH TAKE I (FOR STUDENTS)

Part I: Mindful Breathing—
Recap from Chapter 3

- Listen to the sound until it softens into silence.
- Switch your attention to noticing your breath.
- Breathe normally, paying attention to the feeling of the breath as it fills your lungs and then flows up and back out the way it came.
- Notice when you lose awareness of the breath and start thinking about something else, daydreaming, worrying, or snoozing.
- Bring your attention back to the breath.
- Return your awareness slowly to the classroom when you hear the sound marking the end of practice.

Part 2: Journaling

- Open your journal carefully while maintaining silence in the classroom.
- Describe, with words or pictures, your experience during Take I. (Give students a minute or two for this task).
- Close the journal and put it away.
- Return your awareness gently to the classroom.

Simply using this journaling exercise, even just once, will help students internalize their experience with Take 1. Using it more frequently, while keeping the journaling time very brief (maybe just a minute or two), positions mindful writing as a regular part of the activity. Should you decide to practice journaling in conjunction with Take 1 for a specified period of time, such as a month, try varying the journal assignments day by day. Begin by asking students to focus on a particular aspect of Take 1, such as when the sound softens into silence or when they attend to the experience of breathing. Then, on a different day, ask them to write in their journals about the experience of noticing thoughts or returning their attention to the breath. You can also invite them to describe bringing their awareness back into the classroom or write about their experiences of mindfulness.

Journaling serves as a general lesson enhancement applicable to any mindfulness activity. The variations are limitless, but they share a common focus on attending to and communicating about first-hand experience. The following journaling exercises provide samples of classroom-based enhancements for the previously presented Mindful Seeing activity as well as a homework assignment:

JOURNALS AND MINDFUL SEEING (FOR STUDENTS)

Part 1: Observation with Journaling— Lesson Enhancement based on Mindful Seeing from Chapter 4.

- Slowly open your journal, maintaining silence in the classroom.
- Divide a new page into three sections.
- Hold the object in your hands.
- Get to know your object just by looking at it without thinking about it. (Give students 30 seconds.)
- Use the first section to journal, with words or pictures, about your immediate impressions of your object.
- Look more closely and examine the object's characteristics such as its shape, color, texture, and marks.
- Return your attention to looking at your object, if you become distracted.
- Use the second section to journal, with words or pictures, about your impressions of the object now that you've looked at it more closely.

Part 2: Journaling about Observation— Lesson Enhancement based on Mindful Seeing from Chapter 4.

- Place your object in the bag. (Collect the objects and then place all of them on a table.)
- Come up to the table and examine all the objects without touching them until you recognize the one you looked at earlier.
- Pick up the object and take it back to your seat.
- Use the third section to journal, with words or pic-

tures, about your own experience while looking for
your object among all the others.

- Close the journal and put it away.
- Return your awareness slowly to the classroom.

Part 3: Mindful Seeing—
Homework Assignment

- Pick an object you use everyday (a shoe, bag, or something else that you can hold easily in your hands).
- Write about (or draw) what you see when you first
look at your object. (Remind students to write in the
first person and tell them to allot a minute or two for
this task.)
- Take another minute to observe it.
- Add to, or change, your first description (or drawing)
as needed.
- Write about your experience of looking at this object.
Did you see anything new about it? What, if any,
thoughts did you have while looking at it?

The classroom-based lesson enhancement uses journaling
as the methodological support for guiding students to consider the way their observations change over time, from first
glance to close observation. The homework assignment goes
one step further, requiring them to look at a familiar object
with new eyes. The variations build skills sequentially, so students approach their homework knowing how to pay attention
both to their first glance and then to the process of closer
observation. The assignment requires them to look at something they're already accustomed to seeing and notice
whether careful observation leads them to identify new visible characteristics of the object or gives them insights into

their impressions of the object. This activity explores ways in which mindful seeing affects *what* and *how* they see.

Journaling about the experience of specific mindfulness techniques does facilitate occasional "aha" moments of insight and connection. After a while, however, focusing on the experience of participating in structured activities becomes less engaging. When writing about mindfulness in the context of particular activities begins to bore students, try switching the journal assignments to highlight mindfulness of qualities like kindness or generosity.

To explore the quality of kindness, for example, you might begin by including a written component to enhance the suggestion in Chapter 5 that students purposefully notice acts of kindness during the day, as well as opportunities to express kindness. Then direct students to use their mindfulness journals to record one example of each of these three experiences: (1) an act of kindness they observed; (2) an act of kindness they initiated; and (3) a situation in which an act of kindness could have been helpful. It's important to remind students regularly that mindful journaling means recording their own direct experience—how they feel and what they notice—without analyzing, judging, or developing ideas about what happens.

Hold a class discussion about a week into the assignment on journaling about kindness. Ask students whether they view "kindness" differently than they did initially, and if they notice more or less kindness within and around them. Some students are likely to answer in the affirmative. Ask whether their impression reflects an actual increase in ambient kindness or their heightened sensitivity to identifying it. Discuss their responses, keeping in mind that this question doesn't have a "correct" answer.

Next, vary the assignment to highlight different qualities, such as empathy, compassion, patience, or generosity. After several days of focusing on a particular quality, pose the same basic question of whether purposefully paying attention to noticing and experiencing that quality actually increases its quantity or improves students' sensitivity to its presence. If some students find focusing on emotions and qualities frustrating and too abstract, suggest they apply mindfulness to noticing more tangible perceptions like the presence of the color green around them or the sounds outside the window.

Middle and high school students often enjoy more latitude in selecting the focus of their journal entries. It's usually enough to prompt them to choose a specific situation and describe their experience. Students' responses typically range from distinct "mindfulness" incidents, such as "I'm totally aware of writing in my journal right now," to frustration over "not noticing" mindfulness at all. In fact, these apparently opposite responses both reflect mindfulness. Emphasize that acknowledging distraction is as important as recognizing attention. When you check in with students about their journals, be sure to remind them the assignment prioritizes the *process* of paying attention without judging specific outcomes.

Homework intrinsically involves an element of mindfulness in order to remember assignments and complete them on time. Usually, students and teachers prioritize finishing the assignments satisfactorily over observing their experience while doing so. Working with journals guides your students to merge these two levels of awareness. They need to apply mindfulness to journaling and pay attention to their experience.

Mindful journaling involves a lot of trust and confidence among students individually as well as between the class and teacher. At the most basic level, students need sufficient self-trust to apply mindfulness to their own experience. Then they rely on self-confidence as they witness their own experiences by writing about them. They also need to feel safe recording personal experiences in a written format. Ask your students whether they want to share their journal entries directly with you, or simply show you they've completed the assignments. Involving students in making such decisions reinforces everyone's sense of trust and communication.

Kindness Reflections for Students

An alternative approach to journaling about kindness involves adapting the Kindness Reflections for Teachers presented in Chapter 5. The first major alteration involves guiding students to develop, generate, and extend a single goodwill wish on their own, rather than presenting them with a scripted set of wishes. Another difference pertains to students' need for specified boundaries related to sharing goodwill with others. Whereas the adult version relies on personal discretion to select challenging, yet appropriate, recipients of good will, the student version sets limits that direct students to identify emotionally manageable recipients.

The student version clearly guides them to send goodwill to someone toward whom they feel occasional frustration or anger, but with whom they feel safe. This clarification is important because a significant number of students have deeply held antipathy toward people who they perceive as threatening, if not dangerous, in some capacity. It would be inappropriate and possibly harmful in a classroom context to encourage students who have survived abuse to generate good will toward their abusers. Kindness is the essence of this activity, and it is critical to support students' experience of generating and extending it to others as a simultaneous act of kindness toward themselves.

The last major modification concerns the activity's conclusion. Whereas Kindness Reflections for Teachers ends with mindfulness practice, the student version finishes with journaling and, as appropriate, discussion. Appropriate for all ages, the following instructions explain the progression:

KINDNESS REFLECTIONS (FOR STUDENTS)

Part 1: Developing a Goodwill Wish

- Breathe mindfully for a minute. (Mark the time for the students.)
- Imagine that you meet someone, somehow, who promises to grant you a goodwill wish.
- Think about which wish you would want granted.
- Consider whether your wish would also be helpful to others. If not, select a different wish so you have one that you like and that would also be beneficial for different people.

Part 2: Wishing for Yourself and a Loved One

- Notice how you feel as you focus on your wish.
- Send your wish to yourself, silently saying, "I wish that I...."
- Notice how you feel when you receive your wish.
- Think about someone you love.
- Send your wish to that person, silently saying, "I wish that (the person you love)...."
- Notice how you feel when you send your wish to someone you love.

Part 3: Wishing for Others

- Think about someone toward whom you have neutral feelings (like the shopkeeper, bus driver, or mailman).
- Experiment with sending your wish to that person, silently saying, "I wish that (the person for whom you have neutral feelings)...."
- Notice how you feel when you send your wish to that neutral person.
- Consider someone with whom you feel safe, but toward whom you sometimes feel anger or frustration.
- Try sending your wish to that person, silently saying, "I wish that (the person with whom you feel safe, but toward whom you sometimes feel anger or frustration)...."
- Notice how you feel when you send your wish to that person.

Part 4: Written Reflections

- Switch your attention back to mindful breathing. (Give students about a minute.)
- Return your awareness to the classroom.
- Take out your journal and write about your experience developing and feeling your goodwill wish.
- Write about your experience extending your wish, to yourself, a loved one, a neutral person, and a more challenging person.

As the teacher, you'll know how to tailor the class discussion according to the needs and maturity of your students. You can begin by focusing on students' direct experiences while participating in the activity or by inviting them to share the content of their wishes. Or you could examine the meaning of "generating and extending goodwill to others." Let your students' interests guide your approach and emphasis. Younger children are typically more willing to share their wishes openly than their older peers. Middle school students are often interested in exploring the connections among people and might appreciate exploring the implications associated with extending goodwill to others. High school students frequently feel surprised that this classroom-based activity touches their hearts, and they might want to discuss what happened or simply think about it privately.

Depending on your students' responses to the activity, and your curricular aims, you can implement Kindness Reflections for Students as a stand-alone activity or incorporate parts of it into your regular classroom activities as a mindfulness booster. You might set aside a minute before you return a stack of graded tests and encourage your students to send themselves goodwill. Or you could make time to send goodwill to others after learning of a crisis in your community or a natural disaster afflicting people far away. You can also use the same general approach and substitute other qualities for kindness, thereby extending patience or generosity.

Using boosters reinforces students' mindfulness skills and also distributes awareness and manifestation of these qualities throughout the day.

Mindful Listening

Cultivating mindfulness of speech builds on prior experience noticing and writing about thoughts, feelings, and sensations. Mindful speech is about combining awareness of your inner experience with paying attention to your outward expressions. Mindful listening, like mindful journaling, is a precursor to mindful speech.

Begin by attending to others' speech and then to your own. As you listen, try to isolate "hearing" from "interpreting," even to the point of giving the sounds of the words more importance than their meaning. Then listen to the sound and the meaning together, keeping in mind the possibility that your attribution of meaning may not be the same as the speaker's. Look at body language and notice verbal delivery while searching for other clues to the speaker's intended meaning and adjust your own interpretation accordingly. Try to focus your attention on the speaker, and his communication, rather than your reaction to what he says. Just listen, and refocus your thoughts and awareness on listening, should you venture away from that direct experience.

After you listen and attend to the experience of "listening" while someone else speaks, shift your focus to speaking and listening to your own voice. At first when you apply mindfulness to speech, you'll likely do sometime later, after the experience. That's fine, and over time, the gap between speaking and noticing will close.

Eventually you'll strengthen the skills required to listen mindfully in the moment *as* you speak. At that point, notice whether your words accurately match your intended meaning. Try to recognize when your last statement "came out all wrong" or if you "just heard yourself" state the answer to a question that's haunted you for weeks. Then, as you become more sensitive to aligning word choice and meaning, shift your attention to the fit between delivery and meaning. Did the gentleness in your tone of voice match the words you used? Or did you say you "weren't upset" through jaws clenched in anger?

Attending to your experience of noticing consistencies or inconsistencies is far more important right now than analyzing the actual fit. As far as possible, refrain from self-judgment should you notice discrepancies between your intentions and statements. Try to avoid getting caught up in chastening yourself with thoughts like "I can't believe I just said that" or "I'm so mad at myself because I didn't really mean what I said"— and if you do find yourself amid such inward criticism, notice that fact and then kindly and gently redirect your inward attention. Simply notice and recognize, "Oh, I just heard myself say that," or "I meant something different from what I just said." Those are facts, and the basic task of developing mindfulness is to notice them fully.

Once listening to your own speech becomes easier, you'll start making adjustments midsentence when you hear yourself misspeaking. Slow down your speech and pause for breath to facilitate these spontaneous shifts. The following strategies also support developing mindfulness of speech:

- Listen to other people speaking, during faculty meetings or in the lunchroom, and attend to the fit between their words, meaning, and non-verbal messages.
- Pause and breathe before making a verbal reply during an intense interchange.
- Develop a strategy to handle situations in which you realize you're not saying what you meant to say. (It's okay to stop mid-sentence in order to clarify and start again.)
- Focus your awareness on what might be happening in and around someone else when his or her language seems inappropriate for the situation.
- Apply mindfulness to your own experience as you speak and notice whether your speech is aligned with your thoughts, feelings, and sensations.

- Allow the silence to extend a little longer before you respond to a question or comment.
- Notice whether you are fully listening to someone else speak, or whether your attention is drawn in other directions.
- Recognize how you feel when you see that other people are distracted when you're speaking.
- Focus on the full experience of listening to someone else speak rather than waiting for specific information.

Mindful speech supports attuned communication. During a dialogue, when two parties are in sync, their conversation can seem effortless. However, if one or both individuals are distracted, their connection is weakened and the efficacy of their communication diminished. Your ongoing interaction with your class gives you a head start both for developing and practicing mindful speech. Your commitment to doing so naturally fosters opportunities for your students to develop the same skills.

Students and Mindful Speech

The methodology of introducing mindful speech along with mindful listening is ideal in the classroom for two reasons. To begin with, the technique appears normal. You're simply infusing a traditional paired reading exercise with mindfulness. Further, students are less likely to experience unproductive self-consciousness when speaking aloud within a familiar structured format.

Begin by picking written materials your students enjoy and can read easily. However, be sure to find a text with very short paragraphs or sections since students will only have a minute or two to read segments aloud. The benefit of supplying the written materials lies in relieving students of having to find their own words while attending to "how they speak" and "how they experience speaking." Students start by reading aloud, *like they usually do*, in order to familiarize themselves with the activity's format.

From then on, you guide them to focus on different aspects of their experience while speaking and listening. This approach works well with students of all ages, beginning with early readers. The following instructions present the basic technique and provide several variations:

MINDFUL SPEECH (FOR STUDENTS)

Introduction

• Read aloud to each other, taking turns, so that each partner reads a selection (paragraph, poem, or other written content) aloud to the other, whose job is simply to listen.

• Think about your experience *reading aloud* and consider how much you focused on understanding the content (story), paying attention to reading aloud, noticing the listener, and/or anything else.

• Think about your experience *listening* and consider how much you focused on understanding the content (story), paying attention to listening, noticing the reader, and/or anything else.

• Don't worry about whether you "did it right" or not; the idea is simply to reflect on your experiences while reading aloud and listening.

• Tell your partner what you noticed most strongly. (Give students a minute to exchange observations.)

Variation 1: Pacing

- Take turns reading the next selection aloud, only this time read as slowly as possible while still allowing your partner to understand individual words and the overall meaning.
- Take a few seconds after you finish each selection to focus on the experience of reading and listening this time, and notice where you placed your attention—on the task of reading or listening, your reaction to the slow pace, your partner's response, the content, and/or anything else.
- Tell your partner what you noticed most strongly. (Give students a minute to exchange observations.)
- Repeat the basic sequence of taking turns reading aloud and listening, pausing after each selection to reflect on your experience and exchange observations, and, next time, read as quickly as possible.

Variation 2: Tone and Meaning

- Repeat the basic sequence while reading in as flat and unemotional a tone as possible.
- Repeat the basic sequence while reading with as much dramatic flair as possible.

Variation 3: Content, Distraction, and Mindfulness

- Repeat the basic sequence while focusing on understanding the content—as you read and when you listen.
- Repeat the basic sequence while paying attention to tapping your foot quickly, but quietly, on the ground as you read or listen.

- Repeat the basic sequence while noticing your own inner experience while reading aloud and listening.

Students generally appreciate sharing their experiences of the different variations with a follow-up class discussion. They might enjoy a free-form discussion, or benefit from a few leading questions. For example, ask them, "Do reading and listening require attention? If so, how much and what was your experience paying attention to reading aloud and listening?" Or inquire, "Are reading aloud or listening simple and straightforward activities or more complex? And is one easier than than the other?" Ask them which variations were the simplest and which the most challenging.

At the end of the class discussion, comment on whether or not your students naturally applied some variation of the word "mindfulness" in relation to this activity. If so, reinforce the point that this activity, akin to other mindfulness techniques, emphasizes paying attention to what's happening as it's happening. If students didn't make the connection on their own, invite them to consider how they could apply mindfulness to speaking and listening. Finally, remind them how formal techniques develop awareness that, in turn, supports informal application of mindfulness in daily life.

Did They Hear What They Just Said?

Once students begin applying mindfulness to spontaneous speech, it's important to support their efforts by reminding them to focus on "how they speak" and "what they really say." You can do this during class discussions, student presentations, and informal conversations. You can also capitalize on any tendency to speak before thinking and apply one of many strategies that combine behavior management with mindfulness practice.

Initially, use a simple classroom-based strategy built around pausing silently when students speak inappropriately and "without thinking" while you're in the midst of teaching. As soon as you hear the interruption, apply mindfulness to the situation and breathe, waiting for twenty or thirty seconds before you actively respond. Meanwhile, make eye contact with the student who interrupted you so everyone knows *you know* what happened. Placing your attention on the student who spoke creates a sense of safety for the rest of the class as they watch and wait.

Silence is a great motivator, and in all likelihood, the student will immediately offer a self-correction or make some attempt at an apology. In most cases, students speak out "mindlessly" and realize their mistake soon after. As you pause and breathe, you create an opportunity for students' awareness to catch up with their actions. If they don't make this connection, you're already in a position to respond. Taking a pause prepares you for a calm and successful intervention.

The ultimate goal of classroom management is, of course, teaching students how to manage their own behavior. At first this requires learning how to notice their own actions in real-time and then recognizing the precursors for their actions and/or the eventual consequences. The key to success with this strategy is training students to take the time to notice their behavior and make the effort required to correct it. With enough repetition, students become familiar with having a pause after they interrupt, and often internalize the practice. This means that, even outside your classroom, they're more likely to take a brief pause for self-reflection as soon as they realize that they've said something out of line.

With younger or less mature students, you might utilize a variation of this strategy that involves responding to an interruption by providing a prompt to trigger self-correction. This works best after you make eye contact and pause for a breath, and especially when you notice your student looks lost, confused, embarrassed, or defensive. Your prompt can be a gesture, like a nod, or a statement, such as, "The way you said that didn't sound respectful *[or whichever other adjective applies]*; how would you say that in a different way?" Often, students feel relieved when you clearly label their statement as inappropriate and empower them with the chance to make a correction.

Sometimes students have a vague sense they've "crossed the line" between acceptable and unacceptable behavior but they don't know exactly why or how they did so. They understand that acknowledging a mistake is an important skill, but they also know the value lies in understanding what they did wrong. As a teacher, your expectations regarding acceptable speech probably differ from those of your students. They need to follow your lead, but they might need a fair amount of guidance and clarification to do so successfully. Providing detailed prompts gives students valuable input before "it's too late." This strategy improves behaviors by training students to gain confidence in assessing their own actions and responding appropriately.

Focusing students' attention on your own self-awareness and modeling healthy behavior combine to meld mindfulness with behavior management. Consider what happens when your class, as a whole, is disrespectful or misbehaves (without posing any immediate safety concerns). You probably call them on their actions, and they stop whatever they are doing, but everyone feels a growing sense of tension. The students know you're upset and they might even acknowledge their culpability. However, they rarely know what to do next.

There are two main factors influencing this situation and its outcomes—your response and their response—and these factors are linked. The situation is not calm if they're "wound up" and you're "upset." While that condition might be natural, high emotions rarely support conflict resolution. Somehow, everyone has to shift into a mental state more conducive to dealing with what happened and moving on. You can facilitate this process.

Begin by drawing the class's attention to you and your own self-awareness by saying something like, "I feel really *[insert adjective]* right now, so I am going to stop what I've been doing and take a few breaths before dealing with this." Narrating your process models bringing mindfulness to your own mental state and cues them to focus on knowing how they feel. Your lead prompts them to notice their own self-awareness. Making time to breathe and calm yourself before responding models an effective use of pausing during an emotionally intense situation. At the same time, your speech and actions draw the class's attention to the current moment, away from either replaying the earlier experience of getting in trouble or worrying about future consequences.

Speaking to Yourself

Modeling mindful speech provides a roadmap for your students to follow. The same technique also works when you apply mindfulness to your own inner conversation. Most of us have patterns of self-talk that we replay over and over again. Over time repetition of these statements creates habits of speech. They can be silent or audible, constructive or not.

Constructive self-talk reminds us to pay attention in healthy ways that support success. Young children frequently offer an unselfconscious verbal narrative as part of their actions. Older children, adolescents, and adults also use self-directed speech to sustain focus. For example, athletes tell themselves to "focus" before an important play and I mutter, "go slowly" when I'm driving my car on icy roads during a blizzard. Noticing your own constructive self-talk can help you boost its impact—after all, you're only "listening" to what "you know you need to hear."

Attending to unconstructive self-talk is also important, because repeating statements that chip away at confidence, self-esteem, and mental clarity is unhealthy. Applying mindfulness to unconstructive self-talk involves a familiar sequence. First you simply notice what's happening. Then you recognize self-talk as speech, without engaging in the content. Just as you can acknowledge a thought by silently saying "thought" you can recognize inner commentary without reacting. If you are applying verbal labels, you can say "self-talk" or just mentally nod to your inner statements, and let the phrases dissolve.

The process is essentially about creating a space between your awareness and your ideas about yourself and their inner expression. Trying to "talk yourself out of negative self-talk" is impractical because you simply prolong the conversation. Consciously switching your attention from interpreting your own commentary to just noticing it, without elaborating on it, is a more productive approach.

Another option is to say something purposefully neutral or general once you realize you're in the midst of unconstructive self-talk. This technique involves using your speech, either silently or aloud (when you're alone), to move your mind away from focusing on your sense of self. Although positive personal statements appear to be the obvious antidote to negative messages, you remain the central focus of both. In contrast, neutral statements guide your awareness back to your direct, present experience. Remembering and making a neutral statement, once or repeatedly, brings mindfulness to your experience. My favorite neutral statements include "pay attention," or "stay here."

General positive statements are similiarly effective because they also focus the mind away from self-talk. Familiar phrases like proverbs or inspiring comments are examples of such statements. I like to remember and repeat wise words I have learned from my grandmother and various teachers. You can pick your own, and use them as needed, even in public or at school, since this technique involves keeping them private.

Keep in mind the words you repeat are less important than the repetition. Selecting your own words offers a kind of protection when you realize your mind is "taking off" on its own cycle of intense feelings, thoughts, or sensations. Mindfulness practice, under normal conditions, builds the skills that can enable you to utilize this strategy under extraordinary circumstances. In essence, this process is about developing awareness of what's happening in and around you, and training your mind to place your attention constructively and at will.

Applying mindfulness to written and spoken words parlays into more skillful communication. You can hear more when you purposely listen to how someone speaks as well as what is said. Likewise, outcomes tend to improve when you make time to consider how the recipient might read your email message before sending a rapid reply. Mindful speech is not about self-censorship, but it does involve restraint and discipline. As with practicing mindfulness techniques that emphasize experiences other than speech, these qualities develop over time. In this way, cultivating mindful breathing or attending to emotions contributes to mindful speech, which in turn promotes constructive communication—in and out of the classroom.

CHAPTER 9
Full Circle

It matters not what someone is born, but what they
grow to be!
 J.K. Rowling, *Harry Potter and the Goblet of Fire*

TEACHERS GIVE ALL DAY LONG—inspiring classes, meeting students' needs, and working with colleagues. When you use so much energy, it's necessary to recharge your reserves. Otherwise teaching, and the additional responsibilities associated with completing paperwork, grading homework, and participating in meetings, becomes unsustainable. School time combined with a night's sleep accounts for two-thirds of the day, and the quality of that time influences the remaining hours of wakefulness. Fatigue sabotages professional performance and personal relationships; work-related stress undermines health, and, at the other extreme, job satisfaction improves well-being, and alternating between rest and appropriate exertion develops skills and stamina.

The school environment demands a high level of exertion from teachers and students without validating everyone's need for real breaks (much less facilitating them)—except in the early grades. Teaching each day is like running a marathon, except after you cross the finish line and the students leave, there are still a few more sprints after school. And, as coaches will explain, taking a break and resting between events significantly improves overall performance.

Taking Time After School

If you've spent the past seven hours caring for your students and colleagues, it's fruitful to take some time to recharge your own energy before beginning your after-school activities. This needn't add a big chunk onto an already packed day—just a few minutes might make all the difference. Many mindfulness techniques require only a brief interval during which you can shift awareness and attention to facilitate making a comfortable transition.

Perhaps you, like so many other teachers, move from your classroom into tutoring students, coaching a team after school, or picking up your own kids. Such structured activities have a recognizable beginning that is an ideal opportunity for using Take 1. Focus on experiencing the present moment, away from mulling over the earlier portion of the day or planning ahead. If mindful breathing doesn't suit you, look out of the window and practice mindful seeing, or take a walk while attending to movement.

If you manage your own time after school, you have more flexibility in creating a distinct break to mark the transition between teaching and whatever comes next. Taking a brief walk outside can clear your mind. Glancing at the newspaper or reading a book of your choice contrasts with schoolwork. Just as you purposefully allow your mind to relax, remember to nourish your body with a healthy and tasty snack. Drinking enough fluids is even more important. Once you've given your mind and body a break from academic pursuits, you'll focus on your next tasks more effectively and with greater ease.

Caring for the physical space of your classroom is another transitional activity that reinforces a sense of closure to the school day. When you observe your empty room, look for ways to invest a little energy in making the physical environment more conducive for teaching and learning. Bringing beauty into the classroom helps everyone, aesthetically and also symbolically.

A vase of flowers both graces students' participation in class and reminds them that you care about them enough to celebrate your shared space. In addition, the flowers—or other objects—can help you recollect whatever intention you might associate with their presence. Fresh flowers can cue you to take a deep breath so you enjoy their fragrance and nurture mindfulness. Likewise, faded flowers can prompt you to address issues of change and the passing of time with your students. The nature of the object is far less important than the meaning with which you imbue its presence, the impact it has on your experience and the intention you set with relation to it.

A slightly different approach involves placing special (but probably not precious or sentimentally valuable) objects on your desk, like rocks, pictures, or shells, and rearranging them or adding to them daily or weekly. Students notice these displays and welcome the chance to learn more about your non-academic interests and experiences. Another benefit of bringing discretionary items into the classroom is that it fosters communication with—and among—students. For example, a shared appreciation of an item on your desk can initiate conversation with an otherwise hard-to-reach student. Likewise, students can unexpectedly discover their own connections, when a special object sparks a common interest unrelated to curricular content.

Students are also likely to notice when you rearrange something special in the room. At the macro level, you might move the furniture to catch the students' curiosity and attention the next day. Or you could change the posters or even draw new doodles on the blackboard to greet everyone first thing in the morning. Even if you teach in different rooms (as opposed to having your own dedicated space), you can still work with this principle. For example, tuck different postcards into your folders at night so you have new images every few days. Then arrange the cards against the blackboard or on a desk so students can enjoy them as well. These simple strategies enrich the classroom environment for everyone and contribute to a sense of freshness that reduces tedium and fatigue.

Heading Home

Once you leave your classroom and exit the school building, take a deep breath of the outside air and look at the sky—even if an urban skyline means you see only a small sliver. Smell and listen to the environment around you, even if the odors and sounds aren't conventionally attractive. Mark the transition from school to after-school and consciously place yourself in new environments.

A related strategy focuses attention on shifting from inhabiting public spaces at school to private spaces when you return home. Either you've just spent hours sharing a classroom with a group of students or moving through several classrooms and encountering even more students. When you get home, most likely you'll encounter only a few people, if any. Notice this difference and allow yourself time to adjust.

Personal time is important and healthy, whether you prefer to be alone or with others. Even if you have to bring school-work home (as so many teachers do), try to manage your schedule so you have time for yourself. It's not enough to postpone relaxing until the weekend; daily rest is important. Rest does not have to mean sleep. It can involve socializing, exercising, and engaging wholeheartedly in enjoyable activities. Strive to take as much satisfaction in nurturing yourself and your loved ones as you do in supporting your students' growth.

Even if you are lucky enough to be able to leave your schoolwork physically at school, it's still important to make a mental shift and leave school-related thoughts and feelings there as well. Without establishing boundaries and purpose-fully switching your attention to the priorities of home, unfinished mental and emotional business from school can easily saturate personal time. Mindfulness has a role here too, through increasing your sensitivity to noticing your inner experience and your outer environment, while shifting your attention into the present.

Balance and Baselines

When you receive as well as give through your teaching, you're likely to have a sustainable and satisfying career. Of course some days—even weeks or years—are better than others. Teaching makes good sense when you experience a balance, if not a net gain, in overall benefits as compared with costs. A symbiotic relationship between teacher and students promotes sustainability, success, and mutual satisfaction. This means you teach and care for your students, and as a result, they learn academically, socially, and emotionally. Their growth consequently increases your satisfaction and motivation to teach. A safe and stimulating classroom climate is a natural byproduct as well as a contributing factor to this outcome. From this perspective, teaching is hard work, but it's more than worth the effort.

Teacher burnout occurs when there is a net loss, when the costs outweigh the benefits, when the energy going out greatly outpaces the energy coming in, and you feel you have little or nothing left to give. Insufficient support from others, both personally and professionally, and other stressors often combine to accelerate the path toward burnout. Once you realize you're heading in that direction you might feel you've reached the end of the line. At that point, you might wonder, "What now?"

Burnout is serious, and if you're traveling down that path, seeking skilled support is often enormously beneficial. This book can help, but the focus here is on working with the precursors and very early stages of burnout—or, hopefully, helping you to avert that condition altogether.

The desire to increase your success as a teacher, as measured both by student performance and your own sense of fulfillment, affects motivation for personal growth and professional development. There's a lot you can do to support this process with mindfulness, and also with other more traditional approaches. The benefits of mindfulness practice accrue from the use of specific strategies as well as the development of skills that enhance other tried-and-true approaches. There are no simple recipes for success, but mindfulness can enrich the process.

One strategy to increase your sense of contentment with teaching takes advantage of the normal ebb and flow of daily satisfaction. On a good day, you might not have any real desire to consider ways to improve your professional experience. In contrast, you might feel overwhelmed by the need to deal with problems on those not-so-good days. The idea here is to use a good day, or even a just okay day, to prepare for the motivation you will need on the less satisfactory days.

Begin by reflecting on your current situation as a reference point against which to measure future growth. Mindfulness facilitates noticing both aspects of this baseline: your environment at school and your inner experience. Starting with the outer world, consider what works well at school and what doesn't. Think about the physical environment, your relationships with colleagues and students, the schedule and workload, the financial compensation, and the interpersonal support you receive.

Then shift your focus to your inner experience. First think about what feels good for you at school—what you enjoy, take pride in, and appreciate about the situation. Then consider the little things you find annoying or confusing. Remember to apply mindfulness so you simply notice the irritations but refrain from engaging with them. You can go further and purposely contemplate the problems or simply wait until they come to your attention.

At some point, you're likely to notice unconstructive self-talk about school or one of those uncomfortable, highly personal questions that threaten to keep you awake, even after a tiring day. These questions can arise regardless of the level of your contentment. Perhaps, like me, you're familiar with the experience of trying to calm your mind in the evening, only to find yourself in the middle of a mental or emotional snowstorm. Thoughts hammer your mind. "Am I really happy?" "What else can I do to help my students succeed?" "What if

I'm not good enough?" "What if no one recognizes my potential?" "Do I have the right to want more job satisfaction?"

This is the moment you prepared for. You know how to apply mindfulness to thoughts and feelings, and you can do so now. Even if those uncomfortable feelings turn from snowflakes into hailstones, just let them fall around you and watch. Answering these questions in the midst of a blizzard isn't practical, but noticing the questions and gaining insight into their meaning is very useful. Now you have information about your experience on the full range of your satisfaction continuum and you're ready to go deeper.

Meditating on Satisfaction

The next step is to explore the issues at the root of those midnight questions safely and constructively. You can do this any time, although it's best *not* to contemplate the questions below when you're trying to fall asleep. The following instructions show one way to apply mindfulness to considering these issues and the next section explains the methodology:

ANALYTICAL MEDITATION ON SATISFACTION (FOR TEACHERS)

1. Practice Take 5.
2. Practice the Kindness Reflections.
3. Consider the following topics and related guiding questions. (Do so in direct sequence, or separately over several days.)
   a. *Motivation to Teach:* Why did you become a teacher in the first place? How did you feel (emotionally and physically) when you started teaching?

b. *High Points:* What do you now enjoy most about teaching? How do you feel (emotionally and physically) when teaching is satisfying and enjoyable?

c. *Challenges:* What challenges you the most about teaching, now? How do you feel (emotionally and physically) when you experience these challenges?

d. *Outer Change:* Identify something you can do to improve your physical environment or schedule to strengthen the outer conditions that promote greater satisfaction at school.

e. *Inner Change:* Reflect on, and then set an intention to generate, greater mindfulness and other desirable qualities to foster the inner conditions that increase satisfaction at school.

f. *Service:* What do you most want your students to learn from you? How can you best teach them about that?

4. Return to mindful breathing or just allow your mind to rest until you're ready to finish the practice.

The progression above begins with mental preparation, leads to self-reflection, and ultimately shifts attention to serving others. It offers a road map for cultivating and applying mindfulness for your own benefit and eventually to help others. Although you can match the scope of inquiry and planned action to your needs, the two basic themes remain constant—caring for self is the foundation for caring about others, and mindfulness infuses your actions and its outcomes.

The sequence begins with two mindfulness techniques. Take 5 calms the mind and brings your awareness into the present moment. Then the Kindness Reflections orient your attention toward an attitude of caring. The gentleness of this step strengthens your ability to consider one or more potentially challenging topics and related questions. Once you select the focus of your self-reflection, allow your mind to settle with the sample guiding questions or a more personal, relevant inquiry. Rest with the questions and notice as thoughts and feelings come into your awareness.

Rather than looking for answers, just experience whatever arises in the presence of the questions. Gather information by noticing your mental, emotional, and even physical responses to the questions. Give yourself time to see what emerges without trying to organize or judge your thoughts. Then take the next step and consider the meaning of what you notice even as you continue maintaining awareness of your current experience.

Outer change is more tangible than inner change, and so the progression addresses environmental options first. In a teaching context, this often means identifying workable, simple modifications that can help reduce your dissatisfaction and increase your enjoyment in the classroom. Begin with the little things, like: Do you eat enough for lunch? Is your classroom too hot or too cold? Do the lights give you headaches? Then reflect on some of the bigger issues, such as: Can you integrate some of the topics you most care about into an uninspiring but mandated curriculum? Maintain your awareness of your environmental and structural issues even as you consider when—and where—you can take action.

Once you develop at least one way to positively impact your outer environment, shift your attention to working with—but not *on*—your inner experience. The distinction between *with* and *on* points to constructive engagement rather than setting the stage for a inner battle. There are no "quick fixes" for discontent and unhappiness. First, acknowledge the presence of these feelings as the reality of your current experience. Everything changes, and feelings are not indelible facts—which means they will alter over time. Knowing where you are, mentally, physically, and emotionally, right now is the foundation from which to measure change. So, if you feel miserable *right now*, just notice your experience with mindfulness.

Making that simple shift in perspective can initiate massive change. Once you recognize, "Oh, *this is what it's like to feel* unsatisfied," and realize that "*I am not* unsatisfied," you've taken a step toward consciously working with your experience. Just setting an intention to respond to your thoughts and feelings in this manner is highly constructive. Once you develop the confidence and skill in noticing these mental events, you can add another element to your response—perhaps practicing Take 1 or remembering the Kindness Reflections.

These purposeful actions typically support witnessing uncomfortable thoughts and feelings with greater stability and ease. If they work for you, continue with greater confidence. It's also very important to notice if these techniques don't help or simply aren't enough right now. This doesn't necessarily indicate that they aren't useful, it just means you need more support. If so, consider what else you can do to get assistance—including from friends and family, mentors or religious leaders, and physicians or mental health professionals.

Contemplating deeply personal questions combines mindfulness with insight. This type of reflection, or analytical meditation, deepens understanding and brings greater clarity to the process of strategizing future direction. Knowing where you are is the key to figuring out where you want or need to go. Furthermore, noticing the current moment does not prohibit considering what comes next. You can plan mindfully without losing awareness of the experience of planning.

Once you're ready to move on from contemplating or strategizing, allow your mind to rest briefly. Then return your awareness to the present moment at your own pace. Taking a few moments for Mindful Journaling afterward further extends the benefits of this technique. Sometimes, writing or drawing helps clarify the distinct but interconnected experience of noticing the process of self-reflection and developing outcomes based on self-awareness.

Daily Travels

Whereas engaging in a formal analytical meditation requires some dedicated time, reflecting informally on your daily experience takes only a few minutes. The act of applying mindfulness at the end of the day is reminiscent of setting an intention in the morning regarding the coming day. The main difference concerns *orientation*—one technique projects forward, the other casts awareness back over the past. Both involve attending to experience.

Reflecting on the day fosters closure and allows you to catch up, mindfully, with the journey that began early that morning. I like to use a consistent format to structure my daily reflections, in part because by nighttime I'm tired and a standard progression relieves me of the need to construct a unique approach. In addition, I actually find that reusing a practical template doesn't seem to detract from the freshness of daily experience. For me, the consistent format showcases the novelty of each day and provides greater continuity by linking today with yesterday and tomorrow.

The following instructions present a sample progression you can adopt or adapt for use before going to sleep:

SHORT REFLECTION ON THE DAY (FOR TEACHERS)

- Practice Take I.
- Review your experiences during the day, noticing distinct events and transitions, without judging what happened.
- Identify an experience about which you feel pleased with your involvement, and feel that pleasure again.
- Identify an experience about which you feel dissatisfied and consider a more constructive approach for the next time.
- Notice that you are here, now.
- Find at least one thing, however small, for which you can express gratitude.

This brief reflection covers significant territory. As with the Analytical Meditation on Satisfaction, you begin with a minute of mindful breathing to calm the mind and mark the transition to self-reflection. Then you review the day's experiences in your mind's eye just as you would flip quickly through a photo album. Just observe the scenes and experiences you recall, without engaging in a narrative about the content.

There are multiple approaches to reviewing the events of the day. The simplest, and least distracting, is the most traditional—begin with the moment you awoke, and move through the day until your reflection merges into your current awareness. Another option is to notice whether you naturally attend to the day's "events," and if so, shift your focus to hone in on the "transitions" between them. Or play with chronology and review your experience in reverse, moving backward toward waking up this morning. These methods, along with similar variations, introduce new perspectives that support looking directly at "what happened" rather than "thinking about it."

After reflecting on the day as a whole, zoom in on one specific, satisfying experience. Focus on the nature of your involvement and the associated feelings of pleasure and pride. This step is about rejoicing over your achievement, regardless of its scope. The pleasure derived from making a small gesture of kindness is no less valuable than your delight over contributing to school-wide success. The emphasis is on constructive experiences that lead to a healthy sense of inner satisfaction. Rejoicing feels good, and generating that experience through your own actions increases motivation to "do good" again.

You can also bolster motivation to "do good" by briefly considering a dissatisfying experience in order to identify a more constructive approach for use in the future. The idea is to find opportunities for improvement rather than beat up on yourself for mistakes. What's done is done, but considering "how" something turned out poorly can lead to developing other constructive options. It's very important to invest more energy in contemplating desirable alternatives and then move on, rather than wallowing in dissatisfaction. This step is about considering reality, without attaching labels like "failure" since today inevitably fosters possibilities for "doing better" tomorrow.

Next comes clear recognition that *you are right here, right now, in both mind and body.* You can acknowledge your presence as a thought like "Here I am" or with a felt-sense of "being in your body." The idea is to end the reflection experientially through applying mindfulness and paying attention to your awareness of awareness.

The Short Reflection on the Day concludes with directing the mind toward gratitude. You needn't feel enormous thankfulness in these moments, but just finding one thing, one element, no matter how small, and reflecting on it gratefully can have enormous impact on your life.

Intentions for Tomorrow

Intentions extend reflections. Just as setting intentions in the morning informs that day, falling asleep aware of thoughts about tomorrow provides extra time for holding intentions and focusing your attention accordingly. Making a mental commitment to infuse the next day with patience, or generosity or any other constructive quality, also increases the likelihood that you wake up with an awareness of that commitment and remember it through the day.

The reflection practice, introduced in the previous section, offers several options that support setting an intention for the next day. The first is to develop an intention to enhance the quality or skill characterizing the experience that gave you pleasure or satisfaction. For example, if you feel good about the compassionate way in which you handled a difficult conversation with a colleague, you could decide to cultivate similar compassion for that colleague—or another one—tomorrow.

Another possibility is to set the intention around a quality or skill that could have changed your dissatisfying experience into a more satisfying one. If you want to react with anger less quickly when students procrastinate, you could make a mental commitment to practice patience and noticing the arising of angry thoughts before they get enacted. Then, if you fulfill that commitment and realize your intention during class tomorrow, you'll have a new experience over which to rejoice.

Whenever possible, set the intention to strengthen a constructive quality (in the above example, patience) that automatically reduces a less desirable one (angry words or actions), rather than focusing on the less desirable quality directly. Attending to what you hope to increase, rather than what you want to diminish, reinforces the positive. Although the outcomes of strengthening a positive seem similar to weakening a negative, the experience of the process differs, as does the outcome. Intentions that reinforce a desirable quality facilitate a wholesome process as well as constructive results.

In addition to their individual benefits, intentions and reflections positively impact each other through a symbiotic relationship. Intentions provide structure for experiences that in turn provide the fodder for future reflections. Reflections identify specific areas that can guide the direction of future intentions. The back-and-forth relationship provides reference points and opportunities for assessment. You can decide what to focus on and then consider your experience of doing so as you decide what comes next.

Reflections and intentions offer specific opportunities for applying mindfulness to the content and quality of experience. You might find these discrete techniques more compelling than regular mindfulness practice with breathing or other supports, but keep in mind that ongoing training is the basis of successful application. Developing mindfulness isn't like riding a bike—it's an evolving skill that takes time to learn, and constant practice to master.

As you've read in this book, the steps for mindfulness practice are very simple. First, you notice when you're mindful of an object of attention that can range from pinpointed concentration on breathing to the vastness of your inner experience and outer environment. Next you develop the awareness needed to recognize when you lose your focus. Then, when you notice distraction, you purposefully return to the object of your attention and continue practicing mindfulness. Over time, the mutually reinforcing relationship between increasing awareness and heightening attention infuses daily life.

Here and Now

These days, I work with a school-based health center and present health education classes to K–12 students. I continue to provide professional development for educators and work with parents. I still teach standard health content, just as I did at the beginning of my career. But, over time, my emphasis has changed. So too has my experience.

In my early years, I was passionate about health education curricula and I brought mindfulness into the classroom to enhance students' learning. Now, I am excited about mindfulness, and teach health content as a practical and valuable context for honing attention and awareness. I've learned that every academic discipline and any mainstream curriculum can provide appropriate opportunities for mindful teaching and teaching mindfulness. Mindfulness practice is not subject-specific; it generalizes.

As you increasingly embody mindfulness, the practice will increasingly enhance your activities and experiences. The point is to recognize how this type of mental training enriches whatever you do. There's no trick to the process. The key is to develop your capacity for paying attention and improving awareness in the present moment. Noticing what's happening, in and around you, is the process and the outcome.

Mindfulness won't take you anywhere other than here. Living mindfully won't transform you into someone new—you'll simply experience and express your "you-ness" more directly with more creative energy. The same old routines can still structure your day. However, it is more likely that cultivating mindfulness will bring freshness to the experience of familiar events.

Balanced emotions, a calm mind, and greater skill at paying attention all contribute to deeper and more finely tuned awareness. If you bring mindfulness to noticing your body feels tired, you'll still feel tired. But *you* won't *be* tired. Mindfulness opens up an alternative perspective, through your experience, that promotes discernment. Yes, you have feelings. No, they don't fully define you. Your awareness is big enough to notice your feelings and simultaneously witness having those feelings—as well as other events.

Mindfulness is a term that refers to the quality of experience associated with paying attention to experience, directly, and right now. Mindfulness is available to everyone. In principle, it's not proprietary. No one has "ownership" of mindfulness. Anyone can embody mindfulness by applying it. Through doing so, you'll develop your own experience with mindful teaching and teaching mindfulness.

The advantages of practicing mindfulness can appear almost immediately. You'll enhance the quality of your experience and improve your capacity to manage your emotions. Paying attention, honing awareness, and cultivating skills that support caring will enrich your professional and personal development. Kindness, empathy, and compassion are among the means and ends of infusing mindfulness into daily life.

Mindful experience is inherently personal, no matter how much we learn from others or teach to others. Each moment provides an opportunity for attending to awareness in the midst of life. Training your mind is the key to realizing this ever-present possibility. Your choice to cultivate mindfulness is a gift to and from yourself and, by extension, a boon for countless others.

APPENDIX I
Summary Encapsulation

SUMMARY OF THE MAIN POINTS
COVERED IN THIS BOOK

- Mindfulness is about direct experience of what's happening in and around you. It's not about changing the nature of that experience. Rather, it's about increasing the skill with which you live that experience.
- Mindfulness trains attention and awareness to, and in, the current moment. These are skills for lifelong learning. They contribute to academic achievement as well as social and emotional learning.
- Mindful teaching and teaching mindfulness are two sides of the same coin; it's only the emphasis that's different. You, the teacher, can model what you teach. When you do so, you turbo-charge students' learning. Instructing them in specific techniques enhances their growth and helps prepare them for mindful living.

- Mindfulness promotes resilience and enhances social and emotional competence. Mindfulness combined with empathy, kindness, and compassion supports constructive action and caring behavior.
- Living mindfully begets greater mindfulness. The more you practice, the more mindfulness will infuse your experience of life, work, and relationships. It is not a panacea, but it can foster essential skills for solving problems and celebrating solutions.
- Embodying awareness, attention, and emotional balance in the moment is mindful teaching. Sharing techniques that develop these skills with students is the essence of teaching mindfulness.

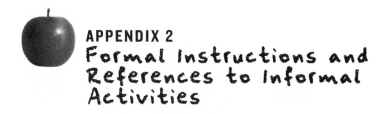

APPENDIX 2

Formal Instructions and References to Informal Activities

Chapter I: Teach as You Learn

FORMAL INSTRUCTIONS

Take 5: Mindful Breathing (for Teachers)

- Breathe normally, paying attention to the feeling of the breath as it fills your lungs and then flows up and back out the way it came.
- Notice when you lose awareness of the breath and start thinking about something else, daydreaming, worrying, or snoozing.
- Return your attention to the breath, with kindness toward yourself and as little commentary as possible.

Chapter 2: Mindfulness in the Morning

FORMAL INSTRUCTIONS

Noticing Thoughts: A Variation on Take 5 (for Teachers)

- Breathe normally, paying attention to the feeling of the

breath as it fills your lungs and then flows up and back out the way it came.

- Notice when a thought (a mental event that involves words) arises.
- Acknowledge the thought by saying "thinking" or "ah yes, a thought" silently in your mind.
- Switch your attention from that thought in particular, back to watching for thoughts in general.
- Continue watching thoughts and acknowledging them inwardly until your session ends.
- As always, be patient, gentle, and kind with yourself.

Noticing Feelings: A Variation on Take 5 (for Teachers)

- Breathe normally, paying attention to the feeling of the breath as it fills your lungs and then flows up and back out the way it came.
- Notice when a feeling or emotional reaction arises.
- Acknowledge the feeling by saying "feeling" or "ah yes, a reaction" silently in your mind.
- Switch your attention from that feeling in particular, back to watching for emotions in general.
- Continue watching emotions and saying "feeling" until your session ends.
- As always, be patient, gentle, and kind with yourself.

INFORMAL ACTIVITIES

Greeting the Day
Intentions
Mini Mindfulness Activities in the Morning

Chapter 3: On to School

FORMAL INSTRUCTIONS

Take 1: Mindful Breathing (for Students)

- Listen to the sound until it softens into silence.
- Switch your attention to noticing your breath.
- Breathe normally, paying attention to the feeling of the breath as it fills your lungs and then flows up and back out the way it came.
- Notice when you lose awareness of the breath and start thinking about something else, daydreaming, worrying, or snoozing.
- Bring your attention back to the breath.
- Return your awareness slowly to the classroom when you hear the sound marking the end of practice.

INFORMAL ACTIVITIES

Sample Strategies for Starting Class
Riddles

Chapter 4: How You See It

FORMAL INSTRUCTIONS

Mindful Seeing (for Students)

- Hold the object in your hands.
- Get to know your object just by looking at it. (Give students about one minute.)
- Look more closely and examine its characteristics,

such as shape, color, texture, and marks. (Give students about two minutes.)

- Return your attention to looking at your object, if you become distracted.
- Place your object in the bag. (Collect the objects and then place all of them on a table.)
- Come up to the table, and examine all the objects without touching them until you recognize the one you looked at earlier.
- Pick up the object and take it back to your seat.

INFORMAL ACTIVITIES

Sample Strategies for Taking Attendance
Mindful Memory
Field of Vision
The Pause and Emotions

Chapter 5: Kindness and Connections

FORMAL INSTRUCTIONS

Kindness Reflections (for Teachers)
- May I feel joy.
- May I heal from pain.
- May I find peace.
- May I gain greater wisdom and skill.

Kindness Reflections for Loved Ones (for Teachers)
- May my loved ones feel joy.
- May my loved ones heal from pain.

- May my loved ones find peace.
- May my loved ones gain greater wisdom and skill.

INFORMAL ACTIVITIES

Guiding Questions for Student Buy-In
Strategies for Settling
Noticing Kindness

Chapter 6: Beads on a String

FORMAL INSTRUCTIONS

Drawing the Mind: Enhancement for Take I
Part I: Current Mental State

- Sit quietly. (Give students about thirty seconds before giving the next instruction.)
- Notice what's happening in your mind: are there thoughts, feelings, or sensations? None, some, or many? Do they remain the same or change?
- Draw a picture of your mental state right now in the left-hand third of your paper. (Give students a minute or so to complete their drawings.)
- Return to sitting quietly.
- Fold the left-hand third of the paper (with the drawing) face-down, so the two remaining blank sections remain face-up covering it.

Part 2: In Silence after the Sound

- Listen to the sound until it softens into silence. (Ring a note on your percussion instrument and wait until there is silence before giving the next instruction.)

- Notice what's happening in your mind now.
- Draw a picture of your mental state in the center third of your paper. (Give students a minute or so to complete their drawings.)
- Return to sitting quietly.
- Fold the center third of the paper (with the drawing) face-down, so now two sections are face-down toward the desk and only one blank section remains visible, face-up.

Part 3: Silence and Mindful Breathing

- Listen to the sound until it softens into silence. (Ring a note on your percussion instrument and wait until there is silence before giving the next instruction.)
- Switch your attention to noticing your breath.
- Breathe normally, paying attention to the feeling of the breath as it fills your lungs and then flows up and back out the way it came.
- Notice when you lose awareness of the breath and start thinking about something else, daydreaming, worrying, or snoozing.
- Bring your attention back to the breath.
- Notice what's happening in your mind now.
- Draw a picture of your mental state in the right-hand third of your paper. (Give students a minute to complete their drawings.)
- Return your awareness slowly to the classroom when you hear the sound marking the end of practice.
- Unfold the paper so the drawings in all three sections are visible.

Mindful Eating (for Students)

Each step can last around fifteen to sixty seconds, or can be varied as suits you.

- Pick up another edible treat.
- Look at it closely and smell it.
- Place the treat in your mouth without chewing it.
- Become familiar with the treat in your mouth—how does it taste and feel?
- Pay attention to the experience of chewing and swallowing.
- Notice the aftertaste and any other sensations in your mouth that follow swallowing.
- Return your attention to the classroom.

Noticing Thoughts (for Students)

- Breathe normally, paying attention to the feeling of the breath as it fills your lungs and then flows up and back out the way it came.
- Notice when a thought arises.
- Acknowledge the thought, perhaps by saying "thinking" silently in your mind.
- Switch your attention from that thought in particular, back to watching for thoughts in general.
- Continue watching and acknowledging thoughts until your session ends.
- Be patient, gentle, and kind with yourself.

Noticing Gaps (for Students)

- Breathe normally, paying attention to the feeling of the breath as it fills your lungs and then flows up and back out the way it came.
- Notice when a thought arises.

- Acknowledge the thought, perhaps by saying "thinking" silently in your mind.
- Switch your attention back to watching for thoughts in general.
- Notice whether there is any space between switching your attention from inwardly acknowledging a thought or saying "thinking" to watching for the next thought, and then let the space go without labeling it.
- Continue watching thoughts and gaps until your session ends.
- Be patient, gentle, and kind with yourself.

INFORMAL ACTIVITIES

Pausing for Breath
Strategies for Mindfulness Boosters
Mindfulness and Resilience (4-point sequence)

Chapter 7: Body Awareness

FORMAL INSTRUCTIONS

Walking with Awareness (for Students)
- Begin walking slowly within the open area in the classroom, silently and without bumping into others.
- Walk normally among each other, without following any pattern.
- Walk as if you're very tired.
- Walk as if you've just heard the most exciting, wonderful news.
- Walk as if your ankle hurts.
- Walk as if you think everyone is watching you.

- Walk as if you want to delay arriving somewhere.
- Walk as if you want to pass unnoticed in a crowd.
- Walk as if you feel proud.
- Walk as if you don't know where you are (or where you're going).
- Walk while paying attention to every movement you make with each step.

Mindful Walking (for Students)
- Begin walking normally but very slowly while keeping your feet on the taped line.
- Make the smallest movements possible as you walk.
- Return your awareness to the experience of walking if you find yourself focusing on something else.
- Don't worry if you lose your balance and fall off the line, just pay attention while repositioning yourself and continue walking.

Mindful Walking—Attending to the Body (for Students)
Use taped lines, or simply ask your class to walk slowly around the room since they are already familiar with the basic experience.
- Begin walking normally, but very slowly (while keeping your feet on the taped line, if applicable).
- Notice the sensations in your feet, legs, torso, arms, neck, and head—do they feel relaxed, tight, heavy, flexible, or something else?
- Notice your breath—is it fast, slow, deep, or shallow, or are you holding your breath?
- Return your awareness to the experience of walking if you lose focus.

- Don't worry if you lose your balance (and fall off the line), just pay attention while repositioning yourself and continue walking.

Mindful Walking—Developing Awareness with Distraction (for Students)

(Use taped lines for this variation and arrange students in single file so they can follow each other *as closely as possible without touching.*)

- Begin walking normally but very slowly while keeping your feet on the taped line.
- Notice your own movements and sensations.
- Notice if/when you become aware of someone behind or in front of you on the line, and then return your attention to your own movement immediately.
- Return your awareness to the experience of walking if you lose focus.
- Don't worry if you lose your balance and fall off the line, just pay attention while repositioning yourself and continue walking.

INFORMAL ACTIVITIES

Strategies for Reading Multiple Messages
Felt Awareness—Body Scan
Mini Mindfulness Movement Techniques
Strategies for Ending Class

Chapter 8: Mindful Words

FORMAL INSTRUCTIONS

Mindful Journaling with Take I (for Students)
Part I: Mindful Breathing—Recap from Chapter 3
- Listen to the sound until it softens into silence.
- Switch your attention to noticing your breath.
- Breathe normally, paying attention to the feeling of the breath as it fills your lungs and then flows up and back out the way it came.
- Notice when you lose awareness of the breath and start thinking about something else, daydreaming, worrying, or snoozing.
- Bring your attention back to the breath.
- Return your awareness slowly to the classroom when you hear the sound marking the end of practice.

Part 2: Journaling
- Open your journal carefully while maintaining silence in the classroom.
- Describe, with words or pictures, your experience during Take I. (Give students a minute or two for this task.)
- Close the journal and put it away.
- Return your awareness gently to the classroom.

Journals and Mindful Seeing (for Students)
Part I: Observation with Journaling—Lesson Enhancement based on Mindful Seeing from Chapter 4.
- Slowly open your journal, maintaining silence in the classroom.

- Divide a new page into three sections.
- Hold the object in your hands.
- Get to know your object just by looking at it without thinking about it. (Give students 30 seconds.)
- Use the first section to journal, with words or pictures, about your immediate impressions of your object.
- Look more closely and examine the object's characteristics such as its shape, color, texture, and marks.
- Return your attention to looking at your object, if you become distracted.
- Use the second section to journal, with words or pictures, about your impressions of the object now that you've looked at it more closely.

Part 2: Journaling about Observation—Lesson Enhancement based on Mindful Seeing from Chapter 4.

- Place your object in the bag. (Collect the objects and then place all of them on a table.)
- Come up to the table and examine all the objects without touching them until you recognize the one you looked at earlier.
- Pick up the object and take it back to your seat.
- Use the third section to journal, with words or pictures, about your own experience while looking for your object among all the others.
- Close the journal and put it away.
- Return your awareness slowly to the classroom.

Part 3: Mindful Seeing—Homework Assignment

- Pick an object you use everyday (a shoe, bag, or something else that you can hold easily in your hands).

- Write about (or draw) what you see when you first look at your object. (Remind students to write in the first person and tell them to allot a minute or two for this task.)
- Take another minute to observe it.
- Add to, or change, your first description (or drawing) as needed.
- Write about your experience of looking at this object. Did you see anything new about it? What, if any, thoughts did you have while looking at it?

Kindness Reflections (for Students)
Part I: Developing a Goodwill Wish
- Breathe mindfully for a minute. (Mark the time for the students.)
- Imagine that you meet someone, somehow, who promises to grant you a goodwill wish.
- Think about which wish you would want granted.
- Consider whether your wish would also be helpful to others. If not, select a different wish so you have one that you like and that would also be beneficial for different people.

Part 2: Wishing for Yourself and a Loved One
Notice how you feel as you focus on your wish.
- Send your wish to yourself, silently saying, "I wish that I...."
- Notice how you feel when you receive your wish.
- Think about someone you love.
- Send your wish to that person, silently saying, "I wish that (the person you love)...."
- Notice how you feel when you send your wish to someone you love.

Part 3: Wishing for Others

- Think about someone toward whom you have neutral feelings (like the shopkeeper, bus driver, or mailman).
- Experiment with sending your wish to that person, silently saying, "I wish that (the person for whom you have neutral feelings)...."
- Notice how you feel when you send your wish to that neutral person.
- Consider someone with whom you feel safe, but toward whom you sometimes feel anger or frustration.
- Try sending your wish to that person, silently saying, "I wish that (the person with whom you feel safe, but toward whom you sometimes feel anger or frustration)...."
- Notice how you feel when you send your wish to that person.

Part 4: Written Reflections

- Switch your attention back to mindful breathing. (Give students about a minute.)
- Return your awareness to the classroom.
- Take out your journal and write about your experience developing and feeling your goodwill wish.
- Write about your experience extending your wish, to yourself, a loved one, a neutral person, and a more challenging person.

Part 4: Written Reflections

- Switch your attention back to mindful breathing. (Give students about a minute.)
- Return your awareness to the classroom.
- Take out your journal and write about your goodwill experience developing and feeling your goodwill wish.

- Write about your experience extending your wish, to yourself, a loved one, a neutral person, and a more challenging person.

Mindful Speech (for Students)
Introduction
- Read aloud to each other, taking turns, so that each partner reads a selection (paragraph, poem, or other written content) aloud to the other, whose job is simply to listen.
- Think about your experience *reading aloud* and consider how much you focused on understanding the content (story), paying attention to reading aloud, noticing the listener, and/or anything else.
- Think about your experience *listening* and consider how much you focused on understanding the content (story), paying attention to listening, noticing the reader, and/or anything else.
- Don't worry about whether you "did it right" or not; the idea is simply to reflect on your experiences while reading aloud and listening.
- Tell your partner what you noticed most strongly. (Give students a minute to exchange observations.)

Variation I: Pacing
- Take turns reading the next selection aloud, only this time read as slowly as possible while still allowing your partner to understand individual words and the overall meaning.
- Take a few seconds after you finish each selection to focus on the experience of reading and listening this time, and notice where you placed your attention—on

the task of reading or listening, your reaction to the slow pace, your partner's response, the content, and/or anything else.

- Tell your partner what you noticed most strongly. (Give students a minute to exchange observations.)
- Repeat the basic sequence of taking turns reading aloud and listening, pausing after each selection to reflect on your experience and exchange observations, and, next time, read as quickly as possible.

Variation 2: Tone and Meaning

- Repeat the basic sequence while reading in as flat and unemotional a tone as possible.
- Repeat the basic sequence while reading with as much dramatic flair as possible.

Variation 3: Content, Distraction, and Mindfulness

- Repeat the basic sequence while focusing on understanding the content—as you read and when you listen.
- Repeat the basic sequence while paying attention to tapping your foot quickly, but quietly, on the ground as you read or listen.
- Repeat the basic sequence while noticing your own inner experience while reading aloud and listening.

INFORMAL ACTIVITIES

Mindfulness Journals
Strategies for Mindful Speaking
Strategies for Mindful Speaking
Speaking to Yourself

Chapter 9: Full Circle

FORMAL INSTRUCTIONS

Analytical Meditation on Satisfaction (for Teachers)

I. Practice Take 5.

2. Practice the Kindness Reflections.

3. Consider the following topics and related guiding questions. (Do so in direct sequence, or separately over several days.)

   a. *Motivation to Teach:* Why did you become a teacher in the first place? How did you feel (emotionally and physically) when you started teaching?

   b. *High Points:* What do you now enjoy most about teaching? How do you feel (emotionally and physically) when teaching is satisfying and enjoyable?

   c. *Challenges:* What challenges you the most about teaching, now? How do you feel (emotionally and physically) when you experience these challenges?

   d. *Outer Change:* Identify something you can do to improve your physical environment or schedule to strengthen the outer conditions that promote greater satisfaction at school.

   e. *Inner Change:* Reflect on, and then set an intention to generate, greater mindfulness and other desirable qualities to foster the inner conditions that increase satisfaction at school.

   f. *Service:* What do you most want your students to learn from you? How can you best teach them about that?

4. Return to mindful breathing or just allow your mind to rest until you're ready to finish the practice.

Short Reflection on the Day (for Teachers)

- Practice Take I.
- Review your experiences during the day, noticing distinct events and transitions, without judging what happened.
- Identify an experience about which you feel pleased with your involvement, and feel that pleasure again.
- Identify an experience about which you feel dissatisfied and consider a more constructive approach for the next time.
- Notice that you are here, now.
- Find at least one thing, however small, for which you can express gratitude.

INFORMAL ACTIVITIES

Strategies for Taking Time After School
Intentions for Tomorrow

Index

A

abuse, xv–xvii, 46
academic performance, 9, 71, 76
acceptance, 105
after-school programs, 2
aggression, 87–88. *See also* anger
"aha" moments, 49, 74, 100, 138
anger, 4, 38, 107. *See also*
    aggression
  body awareness and, 119
  kindness and, 140
  mindful speech and, 144
  pausing when experiencing,
    67–70
  resilience and, 102, 103
announcements, 90
anxiety, 38, 46
  body awareness and, 112, 123
  resilience and, 102
  before testing, 9
artists, 53
assemblies, 90
athletics, 13, 20, 46, 49, 53
  body awareness and, 111
  memory games and, 60
  self-talk and, 153
attendance, taking, 53–55, 56,
    182

B

balance, 161–64, 174
baselines, 161–64
behavior management, 151–52
best practices, 18
biology, 8
"blinker-vision," 61–63
body awareness, 111–29,
    186–88. *See also* Body Scan
    technique; breath; eating
  distractions and, 112, 122–23,
    125
  reflections before sleep and,
    170
  stress and, 23
Body Scan technique, 113–16,
    188. *See also* body awareness
boosters, mindfulness, 91–96,
    125, 186
brain, 1, 8–9, 38, 68. *See also*
    mind
brainstorming, 121
breath. *See also* body awareness
  cultivating kindness and,
    81–82
  journaling and, 134–35
  memory games and, 59
  Mindful Seeing activity and,
    63
  mindful speech and, 151
  mindfulness boosters and,
    94–95
  noticing thoughts and, 27

resilience and, 102
setting intentions and, 20, 23
"Take 1" mindful breathing,
  44–48, 74, 89–91, 133–35,
  181, 189
"Take 5" mindful breathing,
  14–16, 26–30, 133, 179–80
taking a pause and, 68, 70
"Time In" techniques and,
  92
burnout, 162
buy-in, student, 72–76, 183

C
call-and-response sequences,
  42
child abuse, xv–xvii, 46
chimes, sounds of, 87. See also
  music; sound
classes. See also school
  ending, 126–29, 188
  starting, 40–44, 181
  time before, 39–40
classroom, caring for the physical space of, 159
cliques, social, 102
coffee, 32, 100, 133
community-based presenta-
  tions, 12
commuting, 35–36, 153
compassion, 2, 79, 174. See also
  empathy; kindness
  class discussions about,
    84–85
  journaling and, 139
  setting intentions and, 171
computers, working at, 124–25
concentration, 9, 75. See also
  distractions
  learning strategies and, 79
  memory games and, 59–60
confidence, 139–40

contentment, 83, 162–63
creativity, 50–51, 91, 174
curricula, 10–12, 37–38

D
daily
  readings, 79
  travels, 168–71
dancers, 26
day
  anchoring the, 30–33
  -dreaming, 15, 36, 95
  greeting the, 21, 24, 26,
    180–81
  reflecting on the, 196
decision-making, 37–38
dialogue, 131–32, 146. See also
  words
distractions, 55, 56, 194. See
  also concentration
  body awareness and, 112,
    122–23, 125
  learning strategies and,
    76–77
  memory games and, 59
  mindful speech and, 148–49
drawing, the mind, 93–96, 183
driving. See commuting
DVDs (digital video discs), 12

E
eating, 7, 21, 32–33, 96–101,
  185. See also snacks
e-mail, 154
emergency responders, 40
emotion(s). See also specific
  emotions
  body awareness and, 119
  ending classes and, 127
  journaling and, 139
  managing, xiv–xv, 27–30,
    87–88

mindful speech and, 144, 152

noticing, 28–29, 88–89, 180–81

pausing when experiencing, 67–70

resilience and, 102, 103

self-talk and, 154

setting intentions and, 24–25

shutting down, 103

empathy, 2, 71, 79, 174. *See also* compassion

described, 80

journaling and, 139

envy, 87–88

exams. *See* tests

exhaustion, 22, 38, 157, 174

body awareness and, 112, 119, 123

setting intentions and, 22, 23

experiential learning, 58

eye contact, making, 54–55, 150

F

faculty meetings, 20, 133

farewells, saying, 33, 127–29

fatigue. *See* exhaustion

fear, pausing when experiencing, 67–70

feedback, 109

feelings. *See also specific feelings*

body awareness and, 119

ending classes and, 127

journaling and, 139

managing, xiv–xv, 27–30, 87–88

mindful speech and, 144, 152

noticing, 28–29, 88–89, 180–81

pausing when experiencing, 67–70

resilience and, 102, 103

self-talk and, 154

setting intentions and, 24–25

shutting down, 103

Field of Vision activity, 60–63, 182

flowers, in the classroom, 159

frustration, 4–5, 21, 139

kindness and, 140

resilience and, 102

G

goals, 20–21, 24–26

goodbyes, saying, 33, 127–29

goodwill wishes, developing, 141–43, 191–92

greeting

the day, 21, 24, 26, 180–81

students, 40, 53–55

guest presenters, 12–13

H

health

benefits, from movement, 77–78

education, xvi–xvii, 112, 173

HIV prevention, xiii, 112

home-schooling, 2

homework, 60, 75, 127

journaling and, 135–37

grading, 157

humor, 33

hyper-awareness, 48

I

illness, 101. *See also* health

immune system, 8

impulse control, 9. *See also* emotions

intentions, 19–26, 180–81

commuting and, 35–36

journaling and, 133

matching your clothing to,
31–32
for the next day, 171–73, 196
SEL and, 37–38

J
journaling, 132–40, 168, 189–93

K
kindness, 2, 71–88, 174. *See
also* compassion; empathy
cultivating, 80–84
described, 79–80, 85–87
discussions about, 138
journaling and, 138
mindful speech and, 132
noticing, 84–85
reflections, 140–43, 164–65,
167, 182–83, 191
resilience and, 101

L
labeling, of mental events, 28.
See also noticing
language arts, 13, 38
learning styles, 76–79
listening, 6, 132, 143–45, 147,
148
love, "tough," 80
lunch, 25, 90, 96–100, 166

M
martial arts, 43, 116
mathematics, 13, 38, 121
meditation, xiv, 12, 73
focusing the mind and, 131
posture, 14, 46
on satisfaction, 164–68, 169
memorization, 57–60, 121
memory, 56–60, 66–67, 121,
182
mind. *See also* brain; thoughts

"drawing" the, 93–96, 183
"feeding" your, 100–101
use of the term, 8–9
Mindful Movement tech-
niques, 116–26
Mindful Seeing activity, 63–67,
69–70, 74, 135–37, 181–82,
189–91
mindlessness, examining, 7
"mini mindfulness" moments,
89–91, 123–26, 180–81,
188
modeling, 37–38
movement techniques, 116–26
multitasking, 39, 59
music, 13, 36, 42–43, 44–48, 92.
See also sound
myopia, 60

N
nature tables, 78
neurons, 8
New Year's resolutions, 20
noticing. *See also* witnessing
emotions, 28–29, 88–89,
180–81
gaps, 107–8, 185–86
greeting the day and, 18
riddles and, 48–51
setting intentions and, 19–22
"Take 5" mindful breathing
and, 15
thoughts, 27–28, 106–8,
179–80, 185

O
objectives, 25–26
online education, 12

P
pacing yourself, 39–40
pain. *See also* suffering

kindness reflections and, 81, 88
resilience and, 104, 105
past, replaying the, 105
patience, 19, 20, 21, 23, 139
pauses, 67–70, 90, 145, 150–51, 182, 186
pencils, holding, 49
poems, 42, 79
pregnancy, xiii–xiv
psychology, 115

Q
qualities, intangible, 79–80
quizzes, 77

R
reactions, 5–7, 24–25, 103
reading, 132, 147–48, 193–94
recess, 90
resilience, 101–5, 186
responsibility, xiv, 37–38, 101
rest, taking time to, 22
riddles, 42, 48–51, 181
roll call (taking attendance), 53–55, 56, 182

S
sadness, pausing when experiencing, 67–70
safety, sense of, 46
satisfaction, 164–70, 195–96
schedules, 126
school. *See also* classes
    academic performance, 9, 71, 76
    administrators, 11
    commuting to, 35–36, 153
    curricula, 10–12, 37–38
    programs after, 2
    taking attendance, 53–55, 56, 182
time after, 158–60, 196
seeing. *See* Mindful Seeing activity
SEL (social and emotional learning) curricula, xvi, 37–38
self
    association of thoughts with the, 105
    -awareness, 37–38
    -calming, 102, 103
    -esteem, 23
    -judgment, 105, 145, 166
    -talk, 152–55
settling strategies, 76–79, 183
sex education, xv–xvii, 112
Short Reflection on the Day, 168–71
silence, 43, 45, 94, 183–84
sleep, 14, 17, 157. *See also* sleepiness
    reflection before, 168–71
    rest other than, 161
sleepiness, 48, 55. *See also* sleep
snacks, 96, 99, 158. *See also* eating
sound. *See also* music
    mindfulness boosters and, 92, 94
    silence after, 183–84
speech, mindful, 131–55, 189–95
sports. *See* athletics
stopping, before you start, 39–40
stress, xi, 8–9, 73
    burnout and, 162
    effects of, on the brain, 38
    hormones, 8
    resilience and, 102
    setting intentions and, 23

stopping before you start
and, 39–40
stretching, 125
suffering, 102, 104. *See also* pain

T
Tai Chi, 12, 116
"Take 1" mindful breathing,
44–48, 74, 89–91, 133–35,
181, 189
"Take 5" mindful breathing,
14–16, 26–30, 133, 179–80
teachable moments, xiii–xv, 38,
77
telephones, 14
television, 14
tests, 123
therapeutic groups, 86
thoughts. *See also* mind
mindfulness of, 27–30,
105–10
noticing, 27–28, 106–8,
179–80, 185
"Time In," 91–96
to-do lists, 14
training, 12
transformation, xv, 17
trauma, 46, 104, 115
trust, 139–140
truth, 38, 86

V
Viola, Stephen, xi–xii
vision
"blinker-," 61–63
field of, 60–63, 182

W
waking, process of, 17–18, 24
Walking with Awareness technique, 116–20, 124, 133,
186–88
weight loss, 21
welcome, communicating, 18,
48
win-win equations, xi
witnessing. *See also* noticing
greeting the day and, 18
resilience and, 104
"Take 5" mindful breathing
and, 15
words, mindful, 131–55,
189–95
writing, mindful, 132–40. *See
also* journaling

Y
yoga, 12, 116
youth-at-risk, 80

About the Authors

Deborah Schoeberlein has more than twenty years' experience teaching fifth- through twelfth-grade students, developing curricular materials, providing professional development for teachers, and pursuing freelance journalism. She is a recognized leader in developing the field of contemplative education and has published widely on HIV prevention and other health issues. She lives in Basalt, Colorado, with her husband and two children.

Suki Sheth, Ph.D., received her doctorate from Columbia University in 1999. While pursuing her studies, she worked as a teaching assistant with undergraduate and graduate school students. Since returning to her home in Mumbai, India, Suki has tutored teenagers in physics and math. In her spare time, she takes adult education classes in philosophy and hikes in the Himalayas, exploring the mountains of India, Nepal, and Tibet.

About Wisdom Publications

To learn more about **Wisdom Publications**, a nonprofit publisher, and to browse our other books dedicated to skillful living, visit our website at www.wisdompubs.org.

You may request a copy of our catalog online or by writing to this address:

Wisdom Publications
199 Elm Street
Somerville, Massachusetts 02144 USA
Telephone: 617-776-7416
Fax: 617-776-7841
Email: info@wisdompubs.org
www.wisdompubs.org

Wisdom is a nonprofit, charitable 501(c)(3) organization affiliated with the Foundation for the Preservation of the Mahayana Tradition (FPMT).